PRAISE FOR
Your Someday Is Now!

"Gail Alofsin's lively discussion on how to create a 'personal brand' will make succeeding much easier. Her book is written for regular folks and is well worth reading."

Bill O'Reilly, Anchor
The Fox News Channel

"As a busy mother and wife, corporate executive, humanitarian, speaker, professor, author, and friend, Gail Alofsin 'walks the walk' when it comes to Time Management and Personal Branding."

Larry Cancro, Senior VP of Fenway Affairs
Boston Red Sox

"As a 'blow your hair back' go getter and warm generous soul, with a bottomless pit of energy and spirit; Gail ignites your passion for LIVING your time with her sincere and passionate page turning prose."

Sharon Hoyle Weber, Speaker/Author
Hot in the Pot: A Survival Guide for the Real You in the Corporate World

"I have worked with Gail for 25 years, she is a force of nature, a relentless sales and marketing innovator, and has a generosity of spirit that is as contagious as it is inspirational."

Paul O'Reilly, President
Newport Harbor Corporation

"Combining the wealth of experience she has as a dynamic and successful sales and marketing executive, university professor and sought-after thought leader and speaker, Gail's unique perspective on work life integration and personal branding makes this book a must read for anyone who looks at self-improvement as a priority…which is everyone!"

Larry Gulko, Founder
Harvard Business School CEO Forum

"Gail's skills as an educational and inspirational speaker make her a sought-after teacher, consultant and friend. Her book is a must read for anyone interested in bettering their interpersonal skills and motivation in the workplace. Nobody does it better than Gail."

> Mark L. Stenning, Chief Executive Officer
> International Tennis Hall of Fame

"Few people in our field inspire and motivate at the level of Gail Alofsin. We have been fortunate to have her share both her expertise and passion as part of our international conventions for more than a decade, in the areas of leadership, communication, time management and corporate sponsorship. When it comes to creating that all-important work-life balance and building a strong personal brand, Gail serves as both an effective teacher/trainer and example for us all to follow. Her book should be read and included in the personal libraries of leaders from every field."

> Steven Wood Schmader, CFEE , President & CEO
> International Festivals & Events Association (IFEA World)

"Usually parents are able to appreciate the accomplishments and successes of their children. As a woman religious I have not had the privilege of that experience. Rather, in the past 50 years I have been blessed to share in the successes and achievements of my former students. Such is the case with Gail. Her passion for life and ability to motivate people to be their best is interwoven within the fabric of this book."

> Sister Theresita Donach, Executive Director
> Hugs and Halos

"Gail's sincere and dynamic personal wisdom is a tribute to her personal and professional success. The additional advice she offers comes from interviewing over 100 professionals in the business world. Read this book and take control of your destiny!"

> Patrick Snow, International Best-Selling Author
> *Creating Your Own Destiny* and *The Affluent Entrepreneur*

"Gail's passion and energy for inspiring YOU to be YOUR personal best is enlightening and motivating. Need to jumpstart your day? Turn to any chapter and hold on!"

> Tim Cahill, Vice President, Marketing
> Tornier

"Gail Lowney Alofsin brings a refreshing blend of expertise, imagination, professionalism and passion to everything she does. By sharing her many fascinating experiences and relationships, she invites readers to live life to the fullest."

> Renee Hobbs, Professor and Founding Director
> Harrington School of Communication and Media
> University of Rhode Island

"Gail has served as mentor to many of our students. Her book focused on work life balance and best practices in the workplace will leave of legacy of great advice for both students and professionals – whether you have been in the workplace for a few months or several decades."

> Patrick Leary, Associate Professor,
> Johnson and Wales University

"Gail has the rare combination of intellect, personality and the boundless energy of the sun. Her brilliance and warmth are reflected off of everyone around her."

> Kevin Hunt, President
> Chyten Educational Services of Hartsdale, NY

"I have known Gail in several capacities, parent of a graduate, colleague on the board of a social services agency in Newport, and board member of the school of which I am head of school. In all areas Gail is an honest and earnest presence who always follows through on her promises, and will always take the extra step and apply a creative point of view that only improves the situation at hand."

> Whitney Slade, Headmaster
> St. Michael's Country Day School

"For anyone with too much to do and too little time *Your Someday Is Now! What Are You Waiting For?*, provides a fun, informative and useful guide as to how to get off of the "out of control" treadmill and take back your life. The quotes from a variety of successful people, and Gail's own "Toad Tips" along with an outline for the reader to list their own needs creates an opportunity for us to establish new habits for a less stressful and more productive lifestyle. Many thanks to Gail for taking the time to help us to learn new ways to manage our time and our lives."

> Kati Machtley, Director
> The Women's Summit, Bryant University

"Gail Alofsin has captured the essence of time management, leadership and communication in a good read complete with a plethora of wonderful examples and practical exercises. Follow her advice and you will create greater opportunities for successes in your life. The time to start reading this important book is now!"

Dr. Myra Ellen Edelstein, Associate Professor, Business Studies & Economics
Salve Regina University

"Gail Alofsin led our team through a strenuous program review process with enthusiasm, focus and boundless energy. She has been an amazing advocate for our college and our students as well as the consummate hospitality ambassador for our industry. This book, just the latest in a string of her exciting entrepreneurial adventures, demonstrates her understanding of the importance of communication, time management and leadership as cornerstones of success. Truly a "must read" for anyone interested in creating a personal strategy or building a personal brand while balancing the everyday challenge of work/life integration."

Karen E. Silva, EdD, CHE, Department Chairperson
The International Hotel School, College of Management
Johnson & Wales University

"In *Your Someday is Now*, inspirational speaker, corporate executive, philanthropist, professor and mom Gail Alofsin will cure you of the belief you don't have enough time. Instead, you will discover how to master time, make the most of, not just your time, but your work, your attitude, your actions and your life here on earth."

Lisa Tener, Book Coach and Publishing Expert

"Our conference attendees are still raving about Gail's vibrant keynote! Read this book with a highlighter, add a new best practice to your life every day, week, or month, and watch your productivity soar!"

Christine Staron, Member Networking Consultant, Blue Chip Circle
MassMutual Financial Group

Your Someday Is Now.
What Are You Waiting For?

Book design: LegionThirteen / legionthirteen.com
Printed by: The Matlet Group / thematletgroup.com
Back cover photo: Kathryn Whitney Lucey
Editors: Jill Cooper, Brian Heil, Scott Fraser, Heather Hermanowski,
    Marilyn Lowney, Regina Silvia, and Lisa Tener

Every attempt has been made to properly source all quotes.
Printed in the USA
First Edition

AVIVA PUBLISHING
New York

Published by: Susan Friedmann
Aviva Publishing: avivapubs.com

ISBN# 978-1-938686-60-3
Library of Congress control number: 2013954448

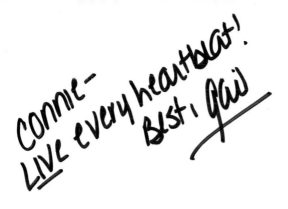

Connie—
LIVE every heartbeat!
Best, Gail

MAXIMIZING YOUR TIME, **YOUR** BRAND, **YOUR** LIFE!

YOUR
SOMEDAY IS
NOW
WHAT ARE **YOU** WAITING FOR?

Gail Lowney Alofsin

DEDICATION

To my husband, John and son, Samuel

My best moments are the gift of time, spent with you.

Contents

Foreword

I first met Gail Lowney Alofsin in 1998 while heading the University of Rhode Island's journalism department after a student told me how much she had learned while serving as Gail's communications and business intern. That student's enthusiasm and endorsement inspired me to meet this dynamic, influential professional—especially because, at that time, I needed to hire someone to teach in our new public relations program.

Meeting Gail on that first occasion, I was faced with a whirlwind of energy and optimism. The student was right. This woman was a born educator. I not only hired her to teach one course, but, in 1999, to create the first public relations courses for our new curriculum. In the time since (15 years, a total of 30 semesters), she has impacted the lives of literally hundreds of students with her positive approach to life, her passion for teaching, and her expertise and knowledge of the field.

Gail is blessed with many gifts, including the gift of aspiration, a yearning to always do more. To this end, she has managed to accomplish a great deal in her young years, following two paths - the "safe" and the "unknown."

In her full time career in sales and marketing for over two decades with Newport Harbor Corporation, the leading hospitality company in New England, Gail has worked with a vibrant team to transform the last four acres of undeveloped waterfront in Newport, Rhode Island, into a mecca of activity and award winning events.

Additionally, Gail is also the President and Founder of AMP! (Authentic Measurable Performance), an educational and inspirational speaking company, delivering hundreds of seminars, presentations, and keynotes since 1999 at both national and international conferences and Fortune 500 companies.

An authority on time management and work/life balance, or as Gail explains it, the "integration of life and work," Gail hits the ball out of the park with this book focused on maximizing your time and enjoying every minute of your life.

With all she has achieved professionally, Gail, rightly, considers her greatest legacy, to be that of being an outstanding mother, wife, sister, daughter, an extraordinary employee, a dedicated, dependable friend, teacher, motivator and a passionate advocate and fundraiser for those less fortunate. She looks beyond herself to create a better world for those less fortunate, locally and internationally.

Looking back on the many years we have known each other, I am struck by how meeting Gail on that fateful day back in 1998 changed my life, as she has often said I have changed hers. It reminds me of one of my favorite beliefs: that there is no such thing as coincidence. In fact, what some see as coincidence, others recognize as opportunity. I'm grateful to have had the opportunity to meet Gail and come to know her as a friend and colleague. It's not a coincidence that you are holding this book in your hands right now. Take hold of the opportunity to learn from the best in the business!

Dr. Tony Silvia
Professor of Journalism and Media Studies
The University of South Florida St Petersburg

PREFACE

We all refer to "Someday."

Someday, I will visit with my family more, spend time with my friends, and absorb the wisdom and history of older friends and family.

Someday, I will start my own company, develop a cool app, learn to play tennis, play more golf, take my vacations, write a letter, read a book, or write a book.

Someday I will teach, someday I will mentor a young person and take time to help those who are less fortunate.

Someday I will call those friends and family I have fallen out of touch with.

Someday I will? YOUR Someday is NOW.

It is never too late to do what you want to do and be who you want to be. Building your brand personally and professionally is a lifelong process versus a singular occasion. Today is *your* day! *Live every heartbeat,* with purpose and gratitude.

Expect more time, own your brand and LIVE your life! Because "Someday," is indeed, NOW.

What are YOU waiting for?

INTRODUCTION

The more knowledge you acquire, the more you realize how much there is to learn in regard to the area of study. This has been the case for me in my study of work and life integration and personal development. I believe that work/life "balance" can be elusive. In a 24/7/365 world, we must learn how to *integrate* our life with our career, becoming more conscious of maximizing our time.

Early in my career, I was inspired by the words of Sir Richard Branson:

"I don't think of work as work and play as play —it's all living. I'm living and learning every day. It's like being at a university, studying a course you are really fascinated by, and in between all that, being surrounded by family and friends."

This insight, reinforced after several flights on his extraordinary Virgin Atlantic Airlines, was a catalyst for doing my very best to integrate a rewarding and successful personal and professional life.

In this book, I share information and best practices accumulated through the observation of and interviews with very busy people. The insight is garnered from my family members and friends in addition to senior managers of companies I have worked with and students that I have had the pleasure to welcome to my classroom at the University of Rhode Island.

Assembling the insights I have personally experienced or learned from others has been a privilege. At the conclusion of some chapters, you will find worksheets you can complete for your own personal development plan. You will also find best practices and success strategies under the caption of *"What are YOU waiting for?"*

The way that you live your life and your time, becomes your personal brand. What do you want to be known for? We have the opportunity to develop our personal and professional brand on a daily basis, embracing a life of learning and leadership.

Knowledge is everywhere – explore your interests and develop your talents. Share your passion! Celebrate the people in your world, every day.

Appreciate the "simple" things, take nothing for granted.

Practice gratitude until it is innate. Offer your "best you" to the world. Be aware of *opportunities* to truly help others.

LIVE Your Time.

At age 12, my son, Samuel, stated – *"Mom, nothing begins until you start."*

It's Your Time, Your Brand, Your Life. *What are YOU waiting for?*

Gail Lowney Alofsin

Chapter 1: The Reality Check
There are No Absolutes

Your Someday is Now.

"The day has 100 pockets if you know what to put into it."

- Friedrich Nietzsche

Time "management" is a myth. Time cannot be managed, it moves forward, stopping for no one. As the adage reminds us, "5:00 will still come at 5:00, no matter *who* you are." Tick tock.

There are few "absolutes."

However, if there is *one* absolute, it is that no matter *who* you are; you have the same amount of time each day. You cannot purchase more time at any price. You can only *organize* and *maximize* the time that you do have.

Time management is *self* management.

8760/1440/365 – You do the Math!

We start each year with 8760 hours – 24 hours in each day. For the illusion of more time, we can break 24 hours into 1440 minutes or 86,400 seconds in a day. But the fact remains, we still have a total of 365 days and these days pass quickly.

How do you use your time? What are your challenges?

Perhaps your time management challenge is being inundated with too many projects, looming deadlines, communication, arguments (internal or external), saying "yes," procrastination, too much paper, or an extraordinary amount of email.

If you had more time, what would you do with it?

Think about what is important to you at this point in your life. Perhaps it is your family (spouse, children, parents, siblings, grandparents, cousins, aunts and uncles), your career (colleagues and clients), friendships (new and old), relationships (personal and professional), intellectual development (higher education, seminars, books, articles), community service initiatives, hobbies or sports.

Defining your "Importance" of the moment will always bring you back to what is most important to you, right now. Stay focused on that.

Reality Check

That's great, Gail, but let's take a reality check. *My* life is very busy.

Your Busy Day!

- Integrating work and home.
- Getting the family ready for the day (children, aging parents, pets).
- Getting to work.
- Organizing and aligning with coworkers and staff.
- Motivating co-workers and clients.
- The volume of work.
- Issues with a boss, supervisor, or colleague.
- Electronic communication.
- Unceasingly rapid changes in technology.
- Responsibilities at home (laundry, cleaning, cooking).
- Family activities throughout the day.
- Volunteer Work (sports teams, charities, boards).
- Job security.
- Deadlines.

Your Someday is Now.

With the proliferation of technology and the pervasive mindset of doing "more, more, more," integrating home and work responsibilities is difficult.

If you are like most people, you start your day with a myriad of things to do. First, you have to get yourself ready for the day, which can be challenging, especially if you did not sleep very well. You may also have the responsibility of getting your family ready for their day – be it your partner, children, aging parents, or pets.

Arriving at your office, it takes time to organize your projects, your day, and your team. Aligning with your co-workers can be interesting, especially if you have people around you who are negative or overly emotional and tend to bring these emotions to work.

Whether you are in charge of a team or a member of one, it is imperative that you exhibit positive leadership skills. Why not? There is no downside to being friendly, motivating, positive and inclusive. Why brand yourself as pessimistic, divisive or arrogant?

My former colleague, Len Panaggio, used to share an expression he adapted from one of his first jobs: *"Leave your bummer at the door and pick it up on your way out!"* Being pleasant and positive in the workplace will save time and inspire a productive culture.

You have many stakeholders to serve during the day. In the business world, you have a wide array – your customers, potential clients, colleagues, management, boards of directors, and the media, to name a few. Serving their needs and concerns can result in unexpected "fire drills" throughout the day.

Our responsibilities at home can also be overwhelming – grocery shopping, organizing, laundry (missing socks!), cleaning, pets, sports and other activities. Coupled with personal appointments and volunteer work, the list can appear to be endless.

The Proliferation of Technology

In high school, we used mimeograph machines to produce our school newspaper. During college, in the early 1980's, we used typewriters to prepare our term papers and exams. The **one** telephone shared in our dormitory room was secured to the wall. We stood in one place while we talked, limiting our ability to multi-task and completely concentrating on the phone conversation. We did not have answering machines, cell phones, voicemail or texting. Roommates shared one telephone number and divided the bill at the end of each month. This is unimaginable for today's generation!

Flash forward to now and the acceleration of technology. It is not slowing down, nor should it. We can achieve so much more with the new devices that increasingly appear on the market. We are more efficient and productive with these technology tools.

Communication and technology will continue to develop at a rapid pace that will be difficult to keep up with. There is so much "out there" that we do not know what we do not know! One of my friends proclaims she has to *"run and run and run,"* just to stay in one place.

Our responsibility is twofold; proper etiquette in regard to the use of technology – personally and professionally –in addition to learning as much as we can about these devices so we can use them to their maximum capability. After all, as soon as we figure out how to use our smart phone, tablet and new computer programs, an updated model appears on the scene.

Moore's Law

In my curriculum at the University of Rhode Island (URI), I recommend that the students read the books and blogs of author and marketing expert, Seth Godin. Seth was a Resident Assistant in my dormitory at Tufts University during my sophomore year. I have great respect and admiration for his business acumen and leadership prowess.

Your Someday is Now.

One of Seth's blogs shared what is referred to as "Moore's Law."

In 1965, Gordon Moore, the co-founder of Intel, predicted that digital memory would double every eighteen months. Every eighteen months!

How much faster can we go? When will enough be enough? As devices become smaller and more portable, how do we balance our personal time to ensure that we "shut off" and take time to enjoy the present moments?

In my teens, Times Square in Manhattan was my annual experience with overload. Now, there is constant activity and engagement, 24/7, and we are in the state of overload every single day, all day. How do we manage all this stimulation – embracing technology yet taking time to breathe?

There is no short or clear answer to this question. Position yourself as a life long learner. Professionally, take the time to keep up with technology, apps and social media that will assist you in being more efficient at your job. Personally, there is so much to be interested in from Facebook to LinkedIn, Flickr to Pinterest and these are just the basics.

Your reality check? *Your* life is busy! Stay focused, embrace technology, have fun and take time to breathe!

What Are You Waiting For?

This might sound crazy, but I like shutting the door and taking a 20 minute power nap…it clears the head and recharges the batteries. I wake up refreshed and ready to kick some a$#!

> Mark Hellendrung, President
> Narragansett Beer

- Write the daily to-do list, then 'star' high priority items
- Go to gym before work.
- Turn email and phone off when writing or working on a big project.
- Get away from office when trying to come up with new ideas.
- When traveling, do your work first on the plane then relax.

> Christopher J. Robertson, Ph.D., Professor
> International Business & Strategy Group
> College of Business Administration Northeastern University

Be conscious about texting in a public situation (i.e. dining room table, restaurant) as it is the same as whispering. It is having private conversation in public.

> Dr. Pam Dipiro, Director of CT
> Dana-Farber Cancer Institute

- Put out clothes and iron if necessary the night before.
- Get minimum of 6 hours sleep a night.
- Review your email and calendar at home with coffee at 6:00 a.m.
- Be nice to people and they are nice back and you have less stress as a result.
- Clean desk once a decade.
- Exercise and eat well.

> Paul O'Reilly, CEO
> Newport Harbor Corporation

Your Someday is Now.

I try to schedule specific times during the day to check email rather than keeping it open and being interrupted by the constant flow of new messages. Times vary depending on meeting schedules, etc., but my goal is to give myself large chunks of time to work on priority projects without being distracted by email messages. I don't go more than a few hours without checking so that I don't miss anything urgent, and of course I make exceptions for days when I'm expecting to be contacted by the media or I suspect senior executives will have frequent questions. I like having the time to concentrate and focus on the more important tasks!

P.S. I'm writing this note on a flight from NY to Dallas. In-flight WiFi does a lot for productivity!

> Jim Andrews, Senior Vice President
> Content Strategy, IEG

As for time management and life balance, there are days that seem impossible. With a very lean communications organization, it helps me to keep looking at the newer trends and outlets, and get comfortable with them so I am not so overwhelmed when we talk about getting our message out. It makes my life a whole lot easier when I can say I tweet, have started to see the value in Google+ and tumblr. It's always a learning experience!

> Nora R. Beger, Director, External Communications and Social Media
> AmerisourceBergen

I used to feel guilty for working during family time. When I evaluated why I was doing it, I realized that it was part out of "necessity" but also part was "habitual." I purchased a private cell number, set up a private email account and now I even have my own, not for work, PC. I am able to choose the times I am going to work rather than to become "sucked in" by the world that is "always on." I have become very selective about where and when I will "plug in" because sometimes a "habitual" email check can generate the "necessity" to respond immediately. I do still allow myself to check in on my days off, but I now I designate the time for it and feel very much more "in control."

> Perry Kessler, Area Sales Leader
> Marriott International

Time Management? It's like a baseball game: one pitch at a time, one out at a time, and one inning at a time.

> Chuck Paiva, General Manager and Co-owner
> Newport Gulls

I have read some great articles and studies showing the inefficiency of trying to multi-task when the human brain is really not capable of effectively doing two things that require thought at the same time. What we really end up doing is "Switch Tasking" where we switch quickly between two or more tasks. This causes us to lose focus on what we were doing, increases stress and anxiety and actually slows down everything you think you are "Multi-Tasking."

When possible, stay focused on what you are doing and try to eliminate the frequent distractions and interruptions that bombard us all day... i.e: Phones, Emails, Texts, Office Drop Ins, etc...

> Randy Schreiber, President
> GutterBrush Guys, LLC

Of course, today's technology allows us to be in touch 24 hours a day and this is an important resource for effective production in doing your job. However, it is crucial that any time away from work spent on your phone, email, or computer is limited to what truly needs your attention immediately... let the things that can wait, wait.

> Luke Sessa, VP, Private Brands
> HH Brown Inc

When it comes to work/life balance, I analyze and decide what is most important at a given time. Sometimes work will require more of my time and energy. This leaves my family feeling a little depleted. I remind them that they will have my undivided attention when we are skiing in New Hampshire for the upcoming weekend or relaxing on a beach at our next family vacation.

> Annie Oster AIC, Lead Training Specialist
> Amica Mutual Insurance Company, Training & Development

Chapter 2: What is Your "All?"
Seize Opportunities to Reinvent yourself

Your Someday is Now.

"Don't tell me the sky's the limit when there are footprints on the moon."

- Paul Brandt

How do you accomplish all that you want to in this world? You start where you are.

Observe people. What are they doing to move forward? What are they doing in order to get it "all" done? The important items in our lives change. We have a plethora of opportunities to recreate ourselves.

It is never too late to be who we might have been.

I am fortunate to have many examples of achievers and positive people in my life. I have learned so much from my parents. One lesson from my mom that I carry with me daily is to "live every heartbeat." We have to enjoy each other, our experiences, and our time together while we have it. A lesson from my father is to do what you say you are going to do. This applies to so many things in life. We have countless opportunities if we stick with the projects that we start. Many of the things worth achieving in life take practice, effort, patience, studying and time.

My brother, Mark, is an OBGYN who has, literally, worked "around the clock" for years. Despite a busy schedule, he plans his time to enjoy the sporting events and activities of his five children, vacation time, exercise and socializing with his friends. His deep faith is an inspiration to many as he places God first and foremost in his life.

My sister-in-law, Kristine, is a full time, extraordinary mother and wife who keeps faith, family, friends and fitness on the forefront as she plans her day. Her home is immaculate and she has a homemade dinner on the table every night.

My sister, Jennifer, has four daughters (inclusive of triplets). At one time, they were all under the age of 3. She works full time as an orthodontist in her own practice, runs triathlons, attends her children's events, maintains a clean house and yes, has a home-cooked dinner on the table almost every night.

Dining together is a gift of time. My mother always prepared a home-cooked meal. Dinner was scheduled for 6:00 p.m. and my father was home for that hour, even if he had to depart for a meeting or return to his office to do paperwork when we were done.

Sharing our day, regrouping as a family, was very important to my mother. Her father died when she was eight years old and she was determined we would spend time together as a family - from dinner in the evenings to activities on the weekend.

She was also adamant about family vacation time. She would go to my father's orthodontic practice, procure the appointment book and cross off two weeks each year. Additionally, she framed every public holiday with a vacation day prior to and following the holiday to lengthen the weekend. Scheduling vacation time offered my father an opportunity to relax and revive - if you can call spending vacation time with 4 children relaxing!

With my own family, we make an effort to eat together several days a week. This offers us an opportunity to share highlights of our day. I am fortunate to have a husband who enjoys cooking and excels at it. John is one of those people who can create scrumptious meals without a recipe and has a spring in his step while preparing baby lamb chops, eggplant towers, curried lentils or a delicious barbecue. *Bon appétit!*

Snack, Recess and Lunch

Dining together offers an opportunity to converse and enjoy each others company – whether we are commencing or concluding our day. While presenting work/life "balance" seminars, one question I am frequently asked is, *"How can we get our family to talk at the dinner table?"*

One suggestion to facilitate conversation is to initiate questions with open ended answers, versus "yes" or "no." When our son, Sam, was younger, I would ask, *"What were three great things about your day?"* Sam would respond, with a smile, *"Snack, recess, and lunch."* I quickly learned to ask, *"What were three great things about your day – in addition to snack, recess, and lunch?"*

We also discovered a game called Table Topics. This game is comprised of cards with interesting questions, evoking thoughtful answers.

I was brought up in a family of four children and it was usually difficult to get a word in edgewise. If you tend to have silence during dining and would like more activity - Table Topics and "Three Great Things" may assist with starting some great conversations.

Capture Time

Capture time so you can spend it on things that are significant to you. Start by reflecting on what is truly important to you, today. Jot a list of items that are significant enough to find time for. This list can become your catalyst to search for those pockets of time.

As you "capture" time, use it wisely. An important item in your world may be spending more time with your family and close friends. It may be enhancing your career, pursuing further education, or learning a musical instrument.

There is no downside in continuing to grow intellectually through staying current about world events while also "studying" subjects you feel passionate about. Education does not stop when you graduate from high school or college. Be a life-long learner and continue the development of your innate interests – hobbies, service to your community, theatre, and sports – whatever captures your interest.

A "non-negotiable" as you capture time is to make sure you are committed to staying healthy through exercise and eating well. A healthy body and mind will always offer you extra time versus hours spent waiting in a doctor's office.

What is Your "All?"

So now it's back to you. What do you want to do? What is your "all?" What is important to you? What are you willing to give up in order to generate more time in your life for the important items?

When you identify and focus on the central items in your life, you will feel accomplished, energetic and fulfilled. Now that, is certainly a step or two, towards your "all."

*ALL – Dictionary.com defines all as *"the entire, the complete, the whole."* You may define your ALL as your capability, purpose, or the way you feel when you are "in your flow."

Captured Time Questions

What do you enjoy doing?

What is your "ALL?"

What are you willing to give up (permanently or temporarily) so you can achieve your "ALL?"

With More Time I Will

Spend more time with my family doing:

Spend more time with my friends doing:

Focus on three new things to enhance my professional growth this year:

1)

2)

3)

Enhance my personal growth with the following action steps this year:

1)

2)

3)

I am going to focus on health each and every day by:

1)

2)

3)

Your Someday is Now.

What Are You Waiting For?

It is far too easy to make the wrong decision about priorities or not to be fully engaged in the moment. How often have you rationalized that staying an extra hour or two at work is an acceptable trade-off versus being home to have dinner with your family? Instead, go home, forget about work and focus on your time together. You can get the extra work done when your children are in bed, that is assuming that the work truly needs to get addressed that day.

Howard A. Samuels, Entrepreneur
Chicago, Illinois

My advice in regard to balancing family and work is to take out your daytimer and plan your week, month or year. First, plug in all your personal commitments, i.e. children's sporting events, activities, workouts, vacation or time off. Then build your work schedule around your personal schedule. This way, your personal life and those things in it come first - as it should be.

Andrew Botieri, Sales & Leadership Trainer
Total Peak Performance

Share audio. Stash away individual ear buds and listen to audio (music, podcasts, TED talks, anything) as a group, both on the road and at home. Use your car's stereo system or an iPod dock to play it out loud for all to hear. Ear buds are so isolating; sharing the experience and having a common reference point of certain songs or audiobooks that you all heard together makes your group a group, instead of just a collection of individuals.

Nancy Staples, Director
Whitesurf Development LTD

• No matter how bad of a day I may have had at work, never, never bring it home.
• Do paperwork after the kids are in bed (when possible).
• Tell my wife and kids that I love them every day.

> Keith J. Miranda, General Manager
> Johnson Brothers of Rhode Island

• Don't schedule meetings during kid's activities/sports.
• When possible work from home one day per week minimum.
• Turn off cable TV.
• Have dinner as a family as often as possible.
• Plan as many family trips as possible each year.
• Pray together as a family.

> Christopher J. Robertson, Ph.D., Professor
> International Business and Strategy Group
> College of Business Administration
> Northeastern University

Identify what your time waster is and learn to eliminate it.
When you are at work…work.

> Marie Y. Cuccia, Director of Sales
> Castle Hill & Resort

Someone once told me – "Work while you are at work and be home while you are at home." I have this in my head and really try to stick to it.

> Amie Kershaw, Vice President, Director of Public Affairs
> Citizens Bank

Your Someday is Now.

Spiritually, work/life balance involves a silent prayer to the Holy Spirit, to keep me in the moment as a reminder I am not in control. With this prayer I come to the realization that life is just one big moment, and we must let life simply "play out."

As a family lawyer, my prayers to the Holy Spirit, seem to be on the way to court, or in a courtroom, when I feel someone has put their family life in my hands, which of course is not really the case. To "Let go and Let God" is easier said than done.

I have told my clients that patience, persistence, and perseverance win cases. One of my clients added peace.

> Michelle Lowney MacDonald, Attorney at Law
> MacDonald Law Firm

I have spent time with many older people and the ones who are happiest don't say - *"I wish I had,"* but instead say, *"I did."* To do is one of the guiding forces of my life.

> Brian Hill, Festival Executive
> Atlanta, Georgia

Leap and the net will appear! When you have the opportunity to take a risk, say this to yourself. There is power in the belief that the world is conspiring in your favor. And being a risk-taker gives you good stories – it is infectious being around people who go for it! Don't be afraid to show your passion and let "leaping" be a part of your personal brand.

> Kendra Wright, President
> Saffire Events

In life, there is no dress rehearsal. You may be asked to do many things all at once, but remember you can only do a few things really well! In your professional and your personal life, always go for quality over quantity.

> Nancy Chandler Drinkwater, VP Client Relationships
> Linkable Networks

Chapter 3: Where does the Time Go?
Back to Basics

Your Someday is Now.

"It's what you learn, AFTER you know it all – That really counts."
- Harry S. Truman

Where does the time go? *Someplace you cannot use it.*

Classic time management divides time into three categories – committed, maintenance, and discretionary. I have taken the liberty of adding a fourth – *squandered time.*

Committed Time

Committed time is comprised of activities involving your immediate and long-term goals. These are the things you have to do, for example – commute to work, plan and organize your project, prepare your budget, write presentations, meet your sales goals, or study. There are also your family obligations – spending time with your parents, or attending a family reunion, a child's sporting event, or a dance recital. As a writer, you have to finish your articles and meet deadlines. As an event producer, conference director, project manager or marketing professional, you have to create a time line to stay on track in order to ensure a successful end product.

Maintenance Time

Maintenance time is focused on maintaining you. This starts with the simplest actions - eating, sleeping, and exercise. We are so busy that there are times we do not eat properly or get sufficient exercise or sleep.

There are your household responsibilities – grocery shopping, cooking, laundry, dishes, and home improvement projects. You are also responsible for automobile maintenance, license renewals, taxes, mortgage payments and monthly credit card bills. You have quite a bit to do to maintain your life.

Maintenance also involves doctor and dental appointments, personal beauty appointments, exercise, yoga, meditation, and other activities that restore your health and well-being.

Taking time to maintain you is critical. It is not self-centered or wasted time.

Discretionary Time

Discretionary time is time set aside to use as you please. We could all use more discretionary time to do what we enjoy doing the most – go on vacation, play 18 holes of golf, take sailing lessons, read a book, enjoy fishing with friends, learn a new skill, join a non-profit board, or read the newspaper cover to cover.

As you hone your time management skills, you will have more time for activities that appeal to you. You just have to be aware of…

Squandered Time

Squandered time is the time you fritter away or use indiscriminately. How do you identify and eliminate time that you may unintentionally and casually give away?

We have all experienced "buyer's remorse" in regard to assuming a new responsibility. *"What was I thinking when I agreed to undertake that project or activity? Why did I say yes…again?"* Many times you were unable to reverse your decision once you made the commitment and did not want to disappoint anyone. Just be aware of this the next time. When you cannot afford to give your time away, simply start the practice of saying *"No, not now. Please ask me again at another time."*

As you review your current schedule, are there appointments you can schedule "to meet" over the phone or Skype versus meeting in person? Are there other people who can attend for you?

When you stop giving away time, you gain more time for the people and actions that have the most positive impact on your life –your family, your friends, and activities you truly enjoy.

It's About Time

Committed Time:

Activities involving your immediate and long term goals.
(Commuting, working, studying)

Maintenance Time:

Maintaining you & your life.
(Eating, sleeping, exercising, household responsibilities)

Discretionary Time:

Time to use as you please.
(You need more of this!)

Squandered Time:

Time that you give-away!

Your Time

Committed Time

Enhancing your future.
List activities involving immediate and long term goals

1)
2)
3)

Maintenance Time

"Maintaining you" checklist. List three things you will focus on this month:

1)
2)
3)

Discretionary Time

Time to use as you please. List things that you would like to do with your free time: (i.e. Create a list of books you want to read, movies you want to watch, places you would like to go…)

1)
2)
3)

Squandered Time

Time that you "fritter" or give away. List current items or activities you plan to reduce or eliminate completely:

1)
2)
3)

Where Should The Time Go? That's up to you!

1) What are your values?

2) What is important to you?

3) What can you give up and replace in your life with free time or a new project?

What Are You Waiting For?

If you have an issue that requires thought, put it aside and give it the appropriate thought. Don't rush – ask questions, do some research, think about it and then deal with it.

Larry Cancro, Senior VP of Fenway Affairs
Boston Red Sox

Book hair, doctor and work out appointments out 6 months in advance. You get a better choice of available times and receive preferred customer treatment if you need to change an appointment. You are also booking "you time" for things that count in your overall health and well being.

At the end of each year, plan a quiet time to review accomplishments from the year. Then list your priorities for the upcoming year. Listing accomplishments is a great way to see how much you have done (ideally, it is done monthly so it takes just a few minutes to complete). When you list annual priorities and you go back to check your list, it is amazing how much you get done.

Angela Moore, President & Founder
Angela Moore

Never book anything on a Monday. Everyone freaks out about the 'Mondays'; don't. Simply wake up, get the kids off to school, brew a cup of your favorite morning beverage, review last week, plan this week, map out a route for the following for days and do something you enjoy. Go for a bike ride. I love to go fishing for an hour or so, the ideas flow in, the plan falls into place and my Mondays make the best weeks possible.

Brendon Walsh, NE Region Sales Manager
Deep Eddy Vodka

Your Someday is Now.

Everyone has a "to do" list. I suggest creating a "Stop doing list." Manage your time better - minimize both your own self imposed distractions and those which come at you from others.

For example, stop feeling you have to answer every email within a nanosecond. Do it on your time, on your schedule. Studies have shown that if you are creating a document in "word" and you respond to a pop up email, it takes an average of 3-4 minutes to get back to your original thought process. There are things we do everyday that impair our productivity. Stop driving over your own speed bumps!

> Larry Gulko, Co-Founder & Chief Strategy Officer
> Cirrus

As you know, managing time is a struggle. Even though we juggle ten chores at once (in the office or home) I try to finish at least one before I accept another. It doesn't always work out in my favor, as each chore, deadline, responsibility is in a constant state of flux, but you have to set your mind on completing that task otherwise you'll never move on.

And I have to write everything down (or type it into my phone). As my to-do list evolves and grows with each responsibility, the feeling of accomplishment I get when I cross something off that list is priceless. You know what I mean!

And if all else fails, take a breath and scoop yourself some ice cream ;) Because in the end, it will get done.

> Annie Sherman Luke, Managing Editor
> Newport Life Magazine
> Newport Wedding Magazine
> Best Read Guide

Don't judge others. No matter how well you think you know someone you are not them. It's not always easy but do your best not to judge.

> Julie A. Montalbano, Sponsorship and Meetings/Events Manager
> Amica Mutual Insurance, Corporate Communications Dept

I heard this from an old boss and it always stuck: You can fit all the things you have to do into 3 categories: water, sand, and rocks. The rocks are the really important things you have to do, the water and sand are things that should get done but aren't as important or time sensitive. By nature, we gravitate toward the "water and sand," when it's the rocks that really need to get moved. Focusing on the "water and sand" makes mud and you get stuck spending time on less important stuff. Focus instead on identifying and moving the rocks and everything else will fall in line.

> Don Troppoli , Vice President Business & Professional Banking
> Webster Bank

Put family first. My wife always tells me – you have to take time to smell the roses. Count your blessings and spend quality time with your children every day.

> Robert Wolfkiel, Vice President and Chief Sales Officer
> Blue Cross Blue Shield of Rhode Island

When the wind of change blows your way, embrace it.

> Liz Zima Cottrell, Director of Development
> Kent Hospital Foundation

"For what does it profit a man if he should gain the whole world and lose his own soul."
- Matthew 8:36.
Paraphrase: Don't work your whole life for what the world values. Think eternally.

> Dr. Mark X. Lowney
> Highland Obstetrics & Gynecology, Inc.

Chapter 4: Busy is Not a Contest!

You are Your Choices

*"If you think you can, you are right.
And if you think you can't, you are also right."*
- *Henry Ford*

One of my favorite books growing up was *The Little Engine That Could* – *"I think I can…I think I can…I think I can… I know I can!"* While this book inspires us to believe that we can do anything and everything, the reality is, we can't.

As we grow older, we learn that no matter how talented or energetic we are, we can only do so much.

"Know" What to "No"

Before you agree to a new position, project or extra-curricular activity, take a look at your schedule. What else have you committed to? When you over commit, nobody wins and you lose the most – sleep, self-esteem, self-respect, and time.

Ask yourself the consequence of saying "yes" or "no" to the requests asked of you. What is the consequence of spending time on a certain project or task versus spending it on something else? This is called your "opportunity cost" and with only 24 hours in a day, you will want to make your choices wisely in regard to how you spend your time.

You have had times in your life when you have said "yes" to too many things, making your plate very full. A full plate is attractive and perhaps, in a sense, comforting. Nevertheless, you only have so much time in a day. If you are consistently inundated with professional and personal extracurricular activities, it will take a toll on your family, your health and your overall well-being.

Learn to say "no." There is a way to decline that does not make the person who is requesting your help feel insulted or hurt.

Saying "NO" Nicely

When you do say "no," why not say it nicely? Think about how honored you are when asked to join a board, chair an event, teach a class, or share your expertise at a conference. After the initial elation, the new responsibility can feel overwhelming.

If you do not have time to fully commit to a new project or initiative, there may be something else you can contribute.

Let's use an event as an example – your college reunion, a local non-profit gala, or a fundraiser for your child's school. If you are asked to be the Chairperson of the event and have to decline, there are other things you can offer to do. Perhaps you can procure a few great prizes for the raffle or silent auction. Do you have access to a caterer or company who will donate food or beverages? You can also introduce the committee chair to people you know who are interested in volunteer work.

Offer to do what you are able to do without any apology. Believe it or not, the person asking for your help has a list of names. When you cannot assume responsibility for a task, he or she will contact the next person on the list.

Be sure to say "no," without a dissertation on how busy you are – *no one cares how busy you are!* We all know people who expound about what they are doing - they are "SOOOO busy." Just agree to do what you are able to do, smile and keep moving. After all, who are you trying to impress?

"Busy" is NOT a Contest!

We all know this person: he or she is always rushing, exhibiting scattered, nervous energy. Too busy to do this…too busy to do that…and still adding more to their plate. Have you been this person?

We wear "busy" as a medal of honor.

Why not make a conscious effort to be busy with beneficial opportunities that present themselves at the right time?

Choose the activities that will add value to your day and to your life.

When possible, choose opportunities you can embrace with gusto versus obligation.

Bless and Release

Before you launch a new project, what are you going to stop doing? No matter how talented or energetic you are, you can only do so much. It is imperative that you "bless and release" existing projects or commitments before you add more to your life.

To bless and release is not only limited to your projects. It is also aligned with the energy you allow into your life, including the people you surround yourself with.

This can be difficult. If a family member is imparting negative energy in your life, it's not easy to "bless and release" him or her. You can, however, limit your time and contact with this person. It may also be difficult to bless and release your friends, boss, coworkers or difficult clients, but you can choose to limit your time and interaction with them as well.

We outgrow some people. This happens naturally. Having once a year, "holiday card friends" is okay.

Be Your Own Hollywood

> *"The world is a great mirror. It reflects back to you what you are. If you are loving, if you are friendly, if you are helpful, the world will prove loving and friendly and helpful to you. The world is what you are."*
>
> *- Thomas Dreier*

There will be moments in your life when people or occurrences may make you feel "less than." People who make you feel this way are not worth your time and interaction. In fact, they will *waste* your time, whether you are simply in their presence or actually interacting with them.

Choose to surround yourself with people who value you, are not envious of your success, and who recognize your worth. Surround yourself with people who do not question or begrudge that you are, indeed, extraordinary.

Try not to waste time obsessing on the success of others to the detriment of your own self-esteem. Do not live trying to be other people. Think about it – is there truly anyone in the world you would completely trade places with? Of course not! Recognize *your* own marvelous. Be *your* own Hollywood. Focus on *your* achievements and blessings.

You have numerous talents and abilities. You have the ability to achieve excellence. Yes, you do.

Addressing Negativity

> *"An eye for an eye makes the whole world blind."*
>
> *- Mahatma Gandhi*

There is a book by Tom Rath and Donald O. Clifton entitled, *How Full is Your Bucket?* This book focuses on how people can make you feel by the simplest of interactions. Do the people you surround yourself with "fill your bucket," bringing positive feelings to your world or do they "dip from your bucket" and leave negativity in their wake?

Your Someday is Now.

Years ago, I worked with a woman known for her ability to "stir it up" and leave a wake of negativity after each of her interactions. In fact, she would carry a clipboard, ranting, *"I am so mad at you…I am SO mad at you; but I am too busy to be mad at you right now – I wrote it down so I do not forget."* Note: You can't make these things up!

There will always be negative people who can bring you down. These people consistently have unkind things to say about other people and make hurtful and untrue remarks behind their backs. If you let these people "empty your bucket," they have won.

When possible, avoid people who have a cloud of negativity around them or people who "deflate your balloon." Negative people attract other negative people and they establish negative clusters. Avoid those clusters.

Make it a habit to attract positive people and situations to your life whenever possible. Be known for a big smile and a positive attitude. Position yourself as a "solutionist"– a problem solver versus instigator! For the most part, people want to spend time with positive people, creating experiences and situations that enrich their world, filling their bucket and yours.

Encourage Others: Be a Cheerleader

> *"Human potential, though not always apparent,*
> *is there waiting to be discovered and invited forth."*
> *- William W. Purkey*

Humanitarian Albert Schweitzer professed, *"In everyone's life, at some time, our inner fire goes out. It is then burst into flame by an encounter with another human being. We should all be thankful for those people who rekindle the inner spirit."*

We never know the impression we are making on another person – whether positive or negative. Think about the people in your life who have encouraged you, excited you, and believed in you. Whenever you have the opportunity - bring out the best in others.

Be aware of how you treat people. My mother always said we may be the only "Bible" people read. What kind of an example are you setting? How are you contributing – personally or professionally – to increasing the self-esteem of a colleague, friend, child, or acquaintance?

Be a contributor. Enter the lives of people you meet and make a difference! In regard to the people who truly mean something to you - family, close friends and colleagues – how difficult is it to be attentive and interested? It is often as simple as putting your mobile phone away and giving your full attention to the person or group you are with.

Everyone is important. Everyone has something to contribute. They may be searching for the inspiration to determine their "calling" or understand their talents. In the workplace, as a manager, leader and colleague, you are charged with bringing out the best in people.

In life, you will be more successful when you help others to become successful.

You are Your Choices

You have so many talents and skill sets. You have the ability to achieve excellence. My friend, Renata Adams, urges, *"Stand tall and give yourself permission to discover and develop excellence."* Renata has inspired people for over 80 years with her wisdom, passion and zest for life. She encourages people to focus on their achievements and to build on them.

In the end, life is what you make it. It starts with what you value. The people and things that matter to you will guide your choices. In the end, you are your choices. They define who you are.

Your Someday is Now.

What choices are you making to add the most value and happiness to your life?

As author Joseph Campbell asserts, *"The privilege of a lifetime is being who you are."*

Go out there and LIVE!

Action Steps – Creativity

Where does your creativity come from?

List three activities you will be add to your life as you create more time. *(For example – tennis, yoga, poetry, art, golf, gardening, sculpture, singing, painting, reading, volunteering, etc...)*

1)
2)
3)

Outline a dream that you would like to fulfill.

List three steps you can take to initiate this dream.

1)
2)
3)

Remember –
You can do ANYTHING – yes, YOU can!

Your Someday is Now.

What Are You Waiting For?

At the end of the day, if you want something done, ask a busy person. The bottom line is that a busy person knows how to get it done.

Larry Cancro, Senior VP of Fenway Affairs
Boston Red Sox

You are 100% responsible for yourself, your relationship to others, and your actions and decisions. Do your best under the circumstances and any limitations (including time) that you are given at each stage. Don't fret as long as you have done so. Don't be afraid to ask for help from friends and family. Operate daily in love and trust God that everything comes together for the good.

Michelle Lowney MacDonald, Attorney at Law
MacDonald Law Firm

My mentor in life has always been my dad. Recently my dad passed away rather quickly learning of his cancer on the day before my parents 50th wedding anniversary. They were scheduled to take the "trip of a lifetime to Italy," a place they always dreamed of going together at this milestone time. Within 5 weeks of his diagnosis he was no longer with us. However, prior to his death, we knew exactly how things should go and what mom should do with her life without him. From the day of his diagnosis, there was one thing that resonated in my heart and my head - I decided that I will live with "no regrets."

So now I live with "no regrets." I don't miss my kids activities, or dinner with family. I never call in sick, I take days off to be with those I love and vacation with them as well. I don't waste time with needless activities or stress. If I want something I get it (well most of the time) and I give more than I receive. I am happy with the decisions I make because I work hard and earn it.

While I miss my dad terribly he taught me so much and for that I can just continue to make him proud by continuing to do my best for my family and others…and yes, that makes me happy and I will not regret it.

Amy R. Haughey, Director, Class & Generational Programs
Brown University - Alumni Relations

The best time management skill I have developed is a mindfulness practice. Often during the day I find I am running from task to task, reactively. I realized a while back that I need to pause, breathe, and ask myself:

1. What am I doing right now?

2. Is there a rush to do any of the 5000 things I have in mind?

3. Do any need to be completed today?

4. Are there any tasks I should do tomorrow?

5. Am I avoiding any important tasks?

I will go through the steps in between each client during the day. I have found that I feel much calmer when I do this and I don't forget important details.

> Daphne Kalaidjian, LICSW
> Mind Body Psychotherapy

To create clarity and success, I journal each morning. It's here that I connect with my inner desires and find "inaccuracies" in thinking that create stumbling blocks to my success. I, then, gain clarity and am able to release any blockages. From these entries, I create my daily affirmation that allows me to realign and step forward into my success.

At night, I fill my blessing bowl with expressions of gratitude I feel for gifts and lessons that I have received during the day as well as joys and blessings that are always in my life. The daily practice of beginning and ending my day this way allows me to embrace life in a state of IN-joy-ment.

> Laura Clark, Spirit & Abundance Coach
> Soul-Wise Living

Don't "*what if?*" your life. Be happy with the decisions you make and don't look back.

> Nicole Bertrand, Acquisition Marketing Manager
> Cox Communications

Your Someday is Now.

Our lives are not static. Things in life come in waves. Waves can bring great bounty or they can wreak great destruction. There is a constant ebb and flow. The trick is to enjoy the bounty when you can and push through the destruction when you must. That has been my experience.

> Mardy Watts Prestley, Esq.
> Doylestown, PA

There is a line in a Dr. Seuss book – *"Any Think Is Possible."* I try to live by this and I am willing to give any idea a chance to come to life. *"We never did it that way"* doesn't work for me. Keep life positive!

> Sister Theresita Donach, CSFN

Don't judge other people's work schedules.

A benefit of being "the boss" is making the rules. I work from home or another off-site location at least three days a week until noon. Sounds leisurely, but it's not. The change in my "workplace schedule" has markedly improved my time management as well as my work/life balance. Quick, mundane house chores during those early hours have replaced the office chatter that would distract if I was in the office. With household duties out of the way early, I am able to fully focus on my son after work. Additionally, I am able to work on "focus-intense" projects like grant writing for three solid hours without staff interruptions. I arrive at the office feeling clear-headed and ready to take on the management elements of my Executive Director role.

When first sampling this new routine, I walked into the office at noon and an employee snipped, *"Where have you been?"* I simply replied, *"I have been being productive elsewhere."* I now afford my staff the same flexibility of schedule, with three simple rules: 1) At least one person must be in the office by 9:00am every day. 2) Get what needs to be done, done and on time. 3) Be at all scheduled meetings.

Our small, hard-working team has been happier and more productive ever since.

> Terri Conners, Executive Director
> NewportFilm

Chapter 5: Got Goals?
Change is the Only Constant

Your Someday is Now.

"This is not your practice life."

- Anonymous

The Spirit of Childhood – You Can Be Anything You Choose to Be

Our mindset as a child is that we can do and be anything. When asked what we are going to be when we grow up, the answer may range from a scientist, doctor, major league baseball player or concert pianist to a famous sensational "someone." Children express their ambitions with bright eyes, exuberant body language, and breathless inflection.

Like most children, I had a vivid imagination. As a young girl, the large rocks I played on at the beach near our house became my "airplane." Dressed in my tropical print bathing suit and a grass skirt, I had a demanding schedule "flying" back and forth to Hawaii daily. I would sing to my passengers (my two sisters and brother) between serving "food" (Sweet pea flowers, daisies, seashells and other inedible items).

The games we played with our neighborhood friends were very simple. Video games did not exist and we had three channels on our black and white television. Going to the movies or going to a friend's house was not something we took for granted – it was an exciting privilege.

The days appeared to be endless. It was a luxury to enjoy time swimming, waterskiing, reading, and exercising with friends in the sunshine. As we grow older, we have the same amount of time, yet it seems to go by so much faster.

When we fall in love for the first time, we see the world with new eyes – "Hello world, where have you been?" A teenager in love sees the world with endless possibilities and passion.

When you evoke that sense of possibility, you can do anything. You can achieve "success," as defined by you. One way to ensure you are on the right path to achieving this success is to set goals.

Got Goals?

Goal-setting is an essential skill to help you develop direction and focus your energy. We have goals and we have dreams; the main difference is that goals have a deadline.

Goals provide us with purpose, vision, and direction. As goal-setting is not something that has been regularly taught in most high schools or universities, many people do not know how to set goals.

Your goal can be as simple as:

- Learn new recipes.
- Schedule and attend workouts at the gym.
- Learn a new musical instrument.
- Take a walk with a friend.
- Read more books.

Goals do not all have to be as enormous as securing a six-figure career right after graduation or procuring an MBA!

Most businesses prepare annual business goals inclusive of overall strategy and budgets outlining revenue and expenses. How many of us commence the year creating personal goals and continue to work towards achieving them once the month of January is long gone?

Overwhelmed? Break the Project into Smaller Bits

Whether it is the beginning of a new year or the beginning of a new project, the feeling of *"How am I going to get it all done?"* can be overwhelming.

You can get started by preparing a plan, checklist, or timeline. You can create this on your computer or on paper. Writing down your ideas and initiatives will clear space in your mind for other items.

Your next step is to review this list. As you start to tackle a few of the items on this list, you will feel a sense of initial accomplishment. If there are tasks you can do without the assistance of others, get these done.

Identify items that require the assistance of others and make appointments with the people who can provide information, insight, or energy.

As you break your project into smaller bits, you will chip away at your goal and eventually bring it to fruition. Remember that the difference between an idea and a goal is that a goal has a deadline – in writing. Don't let it stress you out. Deadlines can be changed; they are not completely black and white. There is a color called grey.

The Road to Kansas

At the beginning of each semester, students are given a syllabus. The syllabus serves as a "map" with an educational destination, outlining what will be taught over the next few months.

Maps assist us with finding our destination in an organized and timely fashion. If you are going to drive from Newport, Rhode Island to Topeka, Kansas, you will need a map. Yes, you can program your GPS, but I personally think you will find it beneficial to review a physical map in order to "see" the end destination in order to determine the best route to take. As you set your course, you may decide to take the highway the entire way. If you are not pressed for time, you may decide to enjoy the beauty of the back roads. Either way, you would review your directions and map prior to getting behind the wheel of a car.

As you set your course, ask for advice from people who have driven from "Rhode Island to Kansas." Seek out people who have accomplished what you would like to. If you do not have direct access to your role models, read about them on the Internet. Where did they start? What challenges did they face as they worked toward their goals? What positive habits and actions enabled them to reach their destination? Take a notepad with you and write their advice down so you can remember and utilize this information.

The Road to Kansas

Envision your professional and personal goals

- Plan your route.
- Seek out other people who have done it.
- Ask for advice.
- Write it down.
- Build momentum.
- Enjoy the journey.

CHANGE is the Only CONSTANT

While goals are important, we are often reminded that change is the only constant: it is inevitable. Goals enable us to control the direction of change in our lives. Goals set our course. We control our sails.

In forming your goals for a balanced life, you may want to evaluate your personal, business, career, and self-improvement aspirations.

This is *your* life and *your* goals. Your ambitions must center around *you*.

The traditional format for business goals is SMART: based on Specific, Measurable, Action-oriented, Realistic, and Time-phased. In order to achieve a business objective, especially when working with a team who rely on your commitment and contributions, fulfillment of SMART goals is crucial to the success of a project.

Think SMART!

Specific: Determine the specific versus general outcome that you desire.

Measurable: Measure and monitor your progress.

Action-oriented: Identify the actions that will contribute to your success.

Realistic: Set goals that are attainable, based on your current skill sets and resources.

Time-phased: Set a date and time to complete your goals. Do not let fear inhibit you from creating a time line- you can always adjust the end date.

Business Goals

Goals: What have you always wanted to do professionally?

1)
2)
3)

Professional Goals

List four benefits you would enjoy as the result of attaining these goals:

1)
2)
3)
4)

SPIRIT Goals!

For your personal goals, I created the acronym SPIRIT goals based on your values.

Spirit goals focus on *your* definition of success, in addition to your passion and interests. They also offer a "reality check" to assess what is realistic at this point of your life. Take time to focus on what inspires you. And, as with all goals, set an end date to accomplish this project or dream.

SPIRIT Goals

Success – How do you define it?

Passion – What do you believe in?

Interest – What excites you?

Realistic – At this point of your life, what is realistic?

Inspired – Who and what inspires you?

Time-phased – When do you expect to accomplish your goal?

About These Goals

• What is your current status?

• What knowledge do you need?

• Who can help you?

• When would you like to accomplish this goal?

Your "Compass" Towards Success

Setting goals will assist with positioning your personal and professional "compass" in the right direction. This will assist you in focusing your energy on achieving accomplishments you will be proud of. North, South, East, West? Go for it!

Goal – noun, the result or achievement toward which effort is directed.
    (Source: Dictionary.com)

Dream – noun, a vision voluntarily indulged in while awake;
        daydream; reverie.
        (Source: Dictionary.com)

What Are You Waiting For?

Each Friday afternoon I invest time by reviewing my calendar for the next two weeks. I review my annual goals and schedule time on my calendar to work on tasks to achieve these goals. This may include meetings with the key stakeholders or blocking out time to work on these initiatives.

Jeffrey P. Gagnon, CPCU, Assistant Vice President Training and Development
Amica Mutual Insurance Company

I regularly use the "Tasks" in Microsoft Outlook and create short notes for each item to remind me of important aspects of the task and next steps to take. This makes it easy to get my head back into each item and move it forward each time it comes up.

John Henley, Chief Operating Officer
Center for Sales Strategy

Whether personal or professional...Set goals. Divide those goals into 3 categories of importance – "Must Do Now Goals," "Sometime Soon Goals," and "On the Future Radar Goals." Create a plan, and do something each day that will bring you closer to reaching your goals.

Natalia Kuziw, Assistant Media Buyer
Deutsch

It may sound crazy, but I "visualize my day." I actually see myself doing one thing to the next. So as I picture the steps, tasks and places I have to be, I make a checklist in my head and then write it down; not always in the nice looking note book. Pieces of paper in your back pocket work just as well, if not better, as you can access them quickly to help guide you along. This process helps me maximize time, be efficient, and not duplicate. And as I get older ;) I am still crazed, but stressed less as I know that it will ALWAYS get done.

Wendy Kopp, Marketing Manager
Panera Bread

Your Someday is Now.

I simply write down my "to do" list on Sunday evening for the week ahead, separating home and business. Furthermore, because I manage people, multiple customers, and vendors, the tasks are placed in "buckets." As the tasks get executed or taken care of, they are simply crossed off. If tasks are not executed they remain for the following week.

I post short, medium and long term goals at my desk. These goals are more personal, for instance, build a wine cellar, sell the condo, pay off truck or house by a such and such date, contribute to a 529 college fund, etc...

I always carry a leather book for my notes rather than rely on my laptop or iPad. It sounds simple and it works for me.

Michael W Lynch, National Sales Executive
Dr Pepper Snapple Group

The idea of "time management" takes on a whole new meaning when you become self-employed. For the first time in my career, I recently left the corporate, cubicle laden world after 17 years to start my own company. Barely 60 days into my new career, the concept of how best to spend my time or maybe more importantly, what to spend my time on has occupied a great deal of my time. I'm a list maker therefore it all starts there for me. I love lists. If there was a career out there of a professional list maker, I'd be the CEO. My challenge is execution of the list. While my process is still evolving, here is what is working so far.

I have a monthly list with everything that I'd like to accomplish during that month. This monthly list has both professional and personal items on it. The monthly list is prioritized using the ABC method; A most important, and so on.

The first thing every morning, I consult my monthly list and move its top priorities to my daily list. The daily list becomes the "Top 10 Things To Do Today." The daily list is also prioritized with the ABC system but also has another step; allocating time to each item. By allocating time to each item, it gives me a snapshot of how much time it will take me to accomplish everything on my daily list. If my daily list time adds up to 20 hours, I know I need to alter something...or it's going to be a long night.

R. Kyle Conway, President
The Sponsor Bureau

Chapter 6: Eat a Frog for Breakfast!
Toad Tips and the To Do List

Your Someday is Now.

"Eat a live frog first thing in the morning and nothing worse will happen to you the rest of the day."

- Mark Twain

Now that you have identified your goals – how do you find time for them?

Author Mark Twain advised, *"Eat a live frog first thing in the morning and nothing worse will happen to you the rest of the day."*

Think about it – what is truly holding you back from "eating" or at least taking a nibble on that big, homely "frog" of a project?

Do you make your "To Do" lists and conquer them by doing the easy tasks first? Whew, that feels good, checking ten action items off your list! However, the "frog," the big project or issue that needs to be addressed, is looming. If you can "eat that frog" earlier in the day, your day will be much more productive.

However, if you attempt to do it at the end of the day, when you are running out of time and your energy is low…watch out!

Making a "to do" list is not enough. Rank your list and focus on the most important items. You may want to start with the traditional "A, B, C, D, E" steps of time management.

"A" are the things you have to do today, if not right now.

"B" are the things you need to get done, but not immediately. "C" are the items that would be nice to do but are not necessary. "D" are matters that can be delegated. "E" are items that can be eliminated if you run out of time.

Classic Time Management

Your "TO DO" list

A – Things you must do, vital or very important:

B – Things you must do, but not urgent:

C – Things to do that are nice, but not necessary:

D – To do items that can be delegated or outsourced:

E – To do items that can be eliminated:

Toad Tips!

1) Do the Tough Tasks First

Take a look at your daily "To Do" list and focus on the tough tasks first. If the project appears to be too big or overwhelming leading you to procrastinate, divide it into smaller tasks. My friend Mark Adams, a former executive at Johnson and Johnson, refers to "To Do" lists as "To Accomplish" lists. Get up, get started, and get it done.

2) Be Productive Everywhere

Learn to be productive everywhere. You will spend time waiting - perhaps for a meeting, doctor's appointment or renewal of your license at the DMV. Pack your purse, briefcase, smartphone, or car with things to read or paperwork to complete. Use this time to clear your email, read an article on your industry, write a letter, or draft a proposal. Stay busy as opposed to idle. When you have something to do, you will not get as frustrated while waiting and you will feel accomplished.

3) Build White Space into Your Day

Build "white space" into your day. Do your best not to book appointments back to back, at least not every day. You may have appointments that go longer than expected. Allow for driving time in the case that you are stuck in unexpected traffic. White space will add respite into your day versus the stress of scheduling every minute of your time.

4) Get Organized

We have so much excess. Take a look at your purse, briefcase, drawers, closet, and desk – our "so much" becomes "very little" because we are no longer aware of what we have.

As a business professional, staying organized for yourself and your clients is the crux of your success, but it can feel overwhelming when you have so many details to manage. Observe successful people and ask them how they stay organized. Absorb their success secrets.

RIBBIT!

For best results, work or study at your high energy time. There are times when your energy level is highest – mornings, evenings, Mondays? (Hmmm, for most people it is Fridays!)

When you experience a random rush of energy, capture this gift. It will help you complete your daily and weekly assignments in addition to working towards achieving your personal and professional goals.

The premise of "eating a frog for breakfast" focuses on doing your toughest tasks first. The end result is that you will have a better day and get more accomplished, mentally and physically, if you start and complete the hardest tasks of your day – be it tadpoles or bullfrogs.

It takes 21 days to start a new habit. If you use self-discipline to get into the practice of "eating frogs," after 21 days it will become second nature.

The result? Productivity.

RIBBIT!

TOAD TIPS!

- Create a daily "To Do" or "Do" list.
- Do the tough tasks first.
- Break projects into smaller tasks.
- Work and study at a high energy time.
- Learn to be productive everywhere.
- Get organized.
- Build "white space" into your day.

White Space (noun) - the unprinted area in a piece of printing, as of a poster or newspaper page, or of a portion of a piece of printing, as of an advertisement; blank space

(Source: Dictionary.com)

What Are You Waiting For?

The best time management advice I ever had was in Naval Supply School fifty years ago. It was to make a list of things to do at the end of every day, for the next day, in priority order. Then, update the list at the end of the next day, etc.

If the list looked too long to get done the next day, then assign some of the items to subsequent days, well in advance. If the list kept growing, and you weren't getting it done, then you either had too much to do, you weren't putting enough time in on the job, or you were wasting time during the day doing things that were not on the priority list.

Sounds simple, but it isn't. It takes practice and discipline, and a willingness to acknowledge your own shortcomings and seek help in improving on them.

> J. Timothy O'Reilly, Retired CEO
> Newport Harbor Corporation

I always prioritize, try to remain calm and organized and always meet deadlines.

> Erminia (Meme) Lindsay, Meeting/Event Planner
> Amica Mutual Insurance Company

In order to keep myself organized and to make sure that I don't forget anything, I write lists! Whether I'm in the office or trying to organize my weekend errands, a list always seems to ease my mind. Being able to cross something off also gives me a sense of accomplishment!

> Brittany Noble, AIC, Training Instructor
> Amica Mutual Insurance Company

Getting up early in the morning (requiring one to go to bed before 10:30pm each weekday) and doing the worst administrative duties first (like paying bills on line, filing bill receipts away, etc.) earns the reward of having fun the rest of the day.

> Victoria Revier, Instructor Coordinator of Medical Administrative Programs
> Bristol Community College

Your Someday is Now.

Something that has always helped me with time management and subsequently work/life balance is making a list each day of all the tasks I need to complete. I scratch each thing off as it's completed and it makes me much more efficient, keeps me focused and accomplished at the end of the day!

Blanca Brown , Senior Account Manager, T&D
Amica Mutual Insurance Company

Prioritize! We've all heard the expression if you want something done, ask a busy person. Whether it's in your personal or professional life, it's a true statement.

As I got older and started a family of my own, I remember asking my mother one Christmas, "How did you get it all done?" She worked. She took care of a husband and family. She baked. She shopped and she wrapped. Her response to me was "you just do it," and she was right. I find when I have more time, I get less done. Whereas the more I have to do, the more I can do. Prioritize. Make lists. Don't get overwhelmed. Take on one thing at a time and do it well.

Susan Tracy-Durant, Director of Creative Services
WPRI 12 & FOX Providence

Write a list. I create a "To Do" list and break it down by area in the city, enabling me to navigate appointments in an orderly fashion. I also stop by busy city areas prior to rush hour. Additionally, I book appointments on similar days back to back and leave myself unplanned time in the day for unexpected things – friends, galleries, work or travel.

Frances Young Fuchs, Actress
Paris, France

The ONLY way that I can manage my time with family, family business, children and extended family is to write EVERYTHING down and leave it where the whole family can see it. I start the week with a sheet of paper (I don't even buy calendars any more) and break it all down: hour by hour, day by day, week by week. In the end it comes down to two things: planning and priorities.

Marie Casale, Publicist
Portsmouth, Rhode Island

Write It Down! Having a to-do list is essential for time-management and I could not function effectively without mine. Once all my tasks are written down, I can then prioritize what needs to be done and track my progress. It allows me to focus my attention and energy on one task at a time instead of constantly thinking about the other things that need to be done. And crossing items off the list just feels so good!

> Kate Chroust, Career Advisor, Career Services
> University of Rhode Island

I have only two TO-DO lists: WORK and PERSONAL. There are occasionally temporary or sub-lists, like (PERSONAL) VACATION PACK, but you get the idea. One constant that has kept me engaged in the "TO-DO" list process has been the great feeling I get when I cross something off! I often add things to my lists that are no-brainers, like "pick up some ice," or "get some gas on the way home," just so I can cross them off. Seeing things eliminated from my list shows progress and makes me want to cross some more things off!

> Chuck O'Connor, CFEE, Director of Corporate Partnerships
> National Cherry Festival

The means to a successful day starts with a healthy mind and attitude. For me, that equals a challenging workout, down to every last repetition. From there, the day's commitments to my husband, children, our schools and charities are achievable.

> Tracy Freese, Real Estate Home Stager
> Charlotte, NC

I'm in sales, so communicating with clients, prospective clients, and partners is crucial to my success. Without a doubt, the single most beneficial concept I use is the 10x10 concept I heard years ago from Gail Alofsin. The idea is simple: "touch" ten prospects or clients by 10:00 a.m. – via phone, email or an in person meeting. However, actually doing it is another thing entirely. I've asked Gail if I could rename her concept to "10x5" but no dice. 10x10 is always #1 on my daily list!

> R. Kyle Conway, President
> The Sponsor Bureau

The key with your "to do" list is to focus your work plan and activity so it stays targeted on the goals or strategies either you or the management team have established that are critical to the success of the venture. By first writing down the top 3 objectives at the top of the page, you reinforce each time the "to do" list is revised with the key goals. Some people work best by revising the list of to do's daily, others weekly or every other day. Whatever works best for the individual is the best method. Some people revise as soon as 50% of the list has been crossed off.

Personally I would try to revise the list on Sunday evenings so I could reflect on what was accomplished the past week and what needs to get done the following week. Also as a President/CEO my key function was to manage, so my lists were focused by area of responsibility for my direct reports. As an example, it wasn't my job to have the month end management financial review complete by Tuesday for a key meeting on Wednesday. However I certainly wanted to follow up with our CFO to make sure we were on track.

At least once a month, chart your actual daily activity in 10-15 minute increments. This will allow you to very specifically determine where your time is being spent. If it's not on accomplishing those key goals, time to rethink your daily activity focus.

Mark Adams, Former International Director, Johnson & Johnson
Former VP of Development, Warner Lambert
Former President, Mystic Pizza

We are all Wonder Women.

In a perfect world, someone else's lack of planning does not constitute an emergency on your part. In reality, no matter how prepared you are, someone else's procrastination and lack of planning can affect you. Just remember - Prior Planning Prevents Poor Performance.

When faced with "emergency," put on your Wonder Woman bracelets and belt, take a deep breath and save the day.

Barbara A. Shea, Tourism Marketing Manager
The Preservation Society of Newport County

Chapter 7: "Real World" Communication
To Be Interesting, Be Interested

Your Someday is Now.

> *"The single biggest problem with communication is the illusion that is has taken place."*
>
> *- George Bernard Shaw*

Your communication acumen will serve to define and develop you as a business professional. Communication is a skill you can improve every day and it starts with awareness of your impact on others.

Your business day operates at an accelerated pace – from the minute you walk in the door at work, or perhaps even earlier, when you turn on your computer, email, or smartphone at home. The days of living in the speed of the "fax machine" are over. We are on double and triple time - in a constant mode of "on."

Effective communication in the workplace will save us time. Even the best business communication tools require patience and focus. From your telephone and appointments to "all that paper," let's review a few time-saving communication tools.

Take Control of Your Phone

How many times have you received a phone message similar to this? *"Hello, this is John, I am calling to (static) …my number is 401-84 (more static)….look forward to (more static)."* Wireless phones, while convenient, are not always "poster children" for clarity.

When you leave a message, be sure to state your phone number twice. For example: *"Hello, this is Gail Alofsin; my phone number is 444-444-4444, that's 444-444-4444."*

You may also want to include your email address when you leave a message, for example: *"If it is more convenient for you to contact me via email, my address is gail4444@blank.com."*

Speak slowly and concisely when leaving your contact information. We have all been the recipients of phone messages comprised of a three to five minute dissertation, followed by the phone number, rapidly recited, at the end of the message. We have to listen to the entire recording again in an attempt to determine the phone number and message. When possible, and if appropriate, follow up on your phone message with an email to the recipient.

On your outgoing recorded message, leave your "signature" by creating your own brand. Are you friendly? Serious? Interesting? Everyone can leave a positive message on his or her outgoing message. This is a prospective employer or client's first impression of you. You want to make sure your message is impressive versus, *"Hey, whassup? Leave a message."*

In addition to a positive message, leave your email address on your outgoing message, especially if it is easier for you to respond to inquiries by email. If you are in the fields of sales or business development, definitely leave your email and, if applicable, your wireless phone number and/or Skype information.

Voicemail Communication

- Leave a brief message.
- Include important details.
- Speak clearly.
- State your phone number twice.
- Include your email address when appropriate.

When you are able to, answer your phone calls in blocks of time, versus the minute they are received. Consolidating your phone calls; for instance, answering them at 9:00 a.m., noon, 3:00 p.m., etc, will serve to increase your efficiency and productivity.

This same practice will work for emails. Replying to emails as they "pop up" can unintentionally expand an email dialogue with back and forth banter; for instance: *"How are you?"… "And you?"*

Email Tips

Email suggestions are readily available – ranging from the advice of business professionals, students, and your own personal experience. While there are hundreds of suggestions and best practices, below are a few that work for me.

1) **Unplug.** Do you best not to be obsessed with email. Your electronic mailbox does not have to be checked every minute or every five minutes. Do you want to live your life on a screen, completely plugged in at all times? Check email at select times throughout the day and live your life, personally and professionally. (Disclaimer: I realize there may be occupations that require email to be checked continuously.)

2) **The One Minute Rule.** When you do check your email, respond immediately if it is important or will simply take you a minute to reply. If the email is more complex, save it and reply during the time of day you have scheduled for email replies.

3) **55/38/7.** Professor Albert Mehrabian's communication model states that 55% of our communication is body language and facial expression, 38% is tone and 7% is our actual words. Thus, we lose 93% of communication when we use email. Most of us have experienced what I have coined "ED" - Email drama! We open the email and may not like what we read. Is it truly something worth 45 minutes of office drama or can you pick up the phone and discuss the email with the sender?

4) **Beware of "SR."** "Selective response" is a pet peeve for many people, and rightfully so. We have to get our work done and often this means that we need information from our colleagues and clients. There are times when an email is answered days or weeks later, or not answered at all. However, if the President of the company sent that same email, most of the recipients would answer immediately! We must do our best to avoid "Selective response" and treat the emails that we do receive with respect – by answering them or picking up the phone!

5) **Be Present.** We attend meetings where people are "present" in the physical meeting yet also tuned in to multiple conversations via their computer, smartphones or tablets. If the culture of the company is one that this is acceptable for internal meetings, then everyone understands that checking texts and emails during meetings is okay. However, if you are in a meeting with clients or in a classroom, turn off your phone. Pay attention to the client, professor or student. This is also important when you are with your friends and family. Unless you have all agreed that smart phones can be used while you are together, put your phone away – avoid "BB" – Blackberry Brush-Off. The "BBD" (Bigger, Better Deal) is not on your phone – it is right in front of you and your presence is required.

6) **File/Save.** File and save emails that are informational or may CYA ("Cover your …") in the future. You can save them in a word file or in your email files in your computer. Create a system that works for you in order to be able to access them again.

7) **Forever Yours.** Just a reminder – once an email is sent, this correspondence lasts forever. Be cautious of sending angry, confidential, or sensitive emails.

8) **Watch Your Grammar.** How are "u" and "LOL" (laugh out loud) is not acceptable for business communication. The first time that I received "LOL" in a business email, I interpreted it as "lots of love" and the person sending it was not the love I was interested in! Complete your sentences, check for spelling and punctuation errors, and keep them brief and organized prior to pressing "send."

9) **Follow Up.** Follow up on the emails that you send. Just because you sent an email does not guarantee that it was received. Your email may have been inadvertently deleted, sent to the wrong address or routed to a spam file.

10) **Shut it Off.** My husband and I both enjoy traveling – especially overseas where email used to be unavailable, slow or sporadic. As his mother is from England, we have spent over two decades vacationing there and in years prior to internet accessibility, we would completely "shut off" for the week or two that we were visiting. Talk about an outstanding vacation! I have also been traveling to Haiti since the early 1980's and the last thing you do in Haiti (in the rare case that the internet in our rural clinic is working!), is immerse yourself in emails.

I could never understand why people constantly check their email while on vacation when they are supposed to be "checked out" and enjoying time off. After all, at work, you are not emailing friends and family all day. Disconnecting and being truly in the moment on vacation will rejuvenate you.

There have been times when I have vacationed during a particularly busy time at work. I have found that I enjoy my vacation better if I check my email in the morning and disconnect until the next morning or two. When email is available, I also like to check in with family and friends if applicable.

In the end, your vacation use of email is up to you. As I mentioned at the beginning of the book, there are no absolutes. You may be at a chapter in your life where you want to stay connected to family, friends, colleagues and clients 24/7. Only you know what is best for you.

With both email and phone calls, do your best not to procrastinate - make the telephone calls and send the emails that will initiate action.

Handling Paper

You may have heard the assertion that the most efficient executives touch a piece of paper once. Hmmm…is this truly possible without a full-time personal assistant?

Most of the paperwork that arrives on your desk will require more than a minute's attention. Chances are, it will be touched more than once.

Manage your paper load. For instance, enter the details of an important date in your electronic calendar, enabling you to discard the original invitation or appointment card. Include the date, time, location, directions, contact name, phone number, what the meeting will be about, and any other important details. If you are able to, delegate the papers on your desk to someone else to read or act upon.

Some people are more comfortable with visible files and papers on their desks. If this is not the case for you or you want to reduce the pile; consider scanning items and creating an electronic filing system that makes sense to you. The system you choose to utilize has to be one that you understand to assist you with maximum productivity.

Start today with baby steps in managing paperwork. It will become a most positive habit.

One Calendar

If you use more than one calendar, you are not alone. Many people have the "family" calendar on the refrigerator at home, the computerized calendar at work, and a "paper" calendar (the "Day Runner" style) for work and personal appointments. Whenever possible, use one calendar. If this is not possible, set a time each week (or more than once a week) when you align your personal and professional calendars to avoid missing or over scheduling appointments. Include time with friends, your personal activities, visits with family, or a child's extra curricular activity. As multiple calendars can be confusing, do your best to get your life organized in one place.

When managing your calendar, make sure you schedule time for driving to and from appointments. You will have appointments that start late or run over. The latter is fine if you are a sales professional meeting with a viable prospect who is willing to give you more time. This is not optimal if you are wasting time by staying longer than necessary to "chitchat." There are also traffic and weather factors when traveling.

Block time in your calendar for exercise and personal time with family and friends. If these items are written in pen on your paper calendar and bold or highlighted in your electronic calendar, the chance of hitting the treadmill or yoga class will be more apt to come to fruition!

In managing your calendar, once again, I remind you to leave "white space" in your day. In addition to unexpected interruptions, you will need time to catch up on your internal paperwork so you are not preventing colleagues from getting their work done. Respect for others in the work place is a tremendous time management tool.

Manage Your Calendar:

- Schedule time for appointments and meetings.
- Use "ink" to block your family time – sporting events, visits with parents, siblings, and children. It's non-negotiable.
- Plan enough time for your personal maintenance – exercise, doctor's appointments, education, and friends.
- Be prepared for unexpected interruptions – leave "white space" in your day.
- Breathe – take time to catch up and enjoy.

Stop, Look, and Listen

One of our earliest childhood lessons is how to cross the street – *"Stop, look, and listen."*

Listening is important; thus the expression, *"God gave us two ears and one mouth, so we can hear twice as much as we say."* We listen and our natural instinct is the urge to reply. You are much more interesting when you are interested in what the other person is saying.

Practice listening. Pay careful attention when another person is talking. Avoid the temptation to "half hear" what the other person is saying. When we "half hear," we may prematurely jump to an interpretation or interrupt our friends, colleagues and acquaintances.

Listening is a very important and powerful communication tool. When we listen with sincerity and focus, the message we send is one of concern, interest, and intelligence. With practice, we can all become excellent listeners. Active listening will always save time.

Listening 101

Think about someone you consider to be a great listener, how do they make you feel?

When you are participating in a conversation, it is natural to be thinking about your response. When you are tempted to interrupt, keep a small pad or piece of paper with you and write down a word or two that will assist you in remembering your thought. Let the person finish; they may address your concern or question as they are talking.

Listening 101:

- Completely hear what the other person has said.
- Do your best to understand what you have heard.
- Ask for clarification if you have questions.
- Interpret what you have understood.
- Respond with the focus on the topic or question.

Communication 101:

- Listen more than you talk.
- Do your best to know your customer, friend, and family.
- Keep your team, boss, family, and friends informed.
- Keep all lines of communication open.
- Communicate your expectations. (Face to face, email, phone, newsletters, memos, personal notes, short meeting, etc...).
- Provide regular and clear feedback.

The Bigger, Better Deal (BBD)

Communication in the "real world" will continue to change and evolve. The basics of Communication 101 remain solid: hone your listening skills, learn what you can about others, share information, become skilled at various modes of communication, let people know what you expect and provide feedback.

True story. When I was young and entering the business world, I was attending a reception with the president of a small local company and his wife, with whom who I was doing business at the time. In fact, I was her client. We were conversing in a group and to excuse himself he boldly stated, *"Excuse me, I am going to go talk to some important people"* and he walked away.

I recall this exchange most clearly as an early lesson of what *not* to do in a social situation.

When you meet with friends, colleagues, or clients; look in their eyes as they speak. Pay attention to their name when they introduce themselves and focus on the conversation. Do your best to avoid looking all around the room or interrupting as they talk. Avoid the BBD (Bigger, Better Deal); visibly searching for someone in the room that you may perceive as more important to talk to.

At a reception or meeting, when an acquaintance approaches you, shakes your hand, and turns to talk to someone else while still holding onto your hand, you do not feel respected. You are, with good reason, insulted.

Be the example. When you are involved in a conversation, listen as if what is being said are among the most important words you have heard all day.

If you are at a reception and have been conversing with a colleague or acquaintance "too long," accompany him or her over to the buffet or towards another person (even if it is a stranger) and kindly state, *"Let's get something to eat"* or, *"Let's meet a new friend."*

Your Someday is Now.

It is equally important to welcome people who are alone at a meeting or reception to enter "your circle." Be warm and welcoming. Many people are shy; invite them to join your group. Initiate conversation and engage them in the discussion. You will meet fascinating new people and learn more than you knew when you entered the room.

Again, as my mother always counseled us, to be interesting, be interested.

What Are You Waiting For?

Unsubscribe from email lists. Open and read an email only once. Deal with it when you open it. Don't come back to it later. Those two work these days.

> PJ Boatwright, VP, Live Media
> Fortune magazine

I try to only handle an email once. I action it and file it.

> Karen Van Dongen, Team Lead
> Unilever

- Do not allow e-mail pop ups. Check e-mails when you have the time allotted to read and reply.
- E-mails sent do not mean e-mails received or read. If it is important, follow up.
- Don't get caught in e-mail or text strings that go back and forth and never end. Respond and end the conversation. A simple, "Chat with you later" or "See you later" generally gets the message across.

> Ellen Ford, President & CEO
> People's Credit Union

I use my in box as my "to do" list. I do not leave work at night until I literally cannot scroll down in my inbox. I do not file or get rid of an email until I have completely closed the loop on it. I then ask anyone I work with that has some type of a request to send me an email on it and I will follow up with it once I return to the office. This is extremely important as in my role I travel a ton and have a lot of requests and items I need to handle, so this helps items from falling through the cracks. In today's world almost everything is digital, I just moved my office and had only 3 file folders with physical paper in them, and everything else is on line, so email is my tool to stay on top of everything and organized.

> Rob Hamilton, Regional Marketing Manager
> Heineken USA

Your Someday is Now.

DEFENSE or OFFENSE??

When I travel on the road and I'm getting bombarded by emails from my desk bound peers, I feel like I am on "email defense." At this point, you have to try to maintain your balance and not let the emails get overwhelming. Time management here is key – from checking in on your blackberry; upon check in at the hotel, after dinner when you get back, in the airport, or on a plane where I'm writing this now (got to love the GoGo WiFi Network!), you need to maximize your time!

When I'm in my office, I can be the person on Offense and send emails out!

> Scott Morin, Vice President, Sales
> Sebago

My best practice is to handle things once and when they come in. Same goes for paperwork, projects, etc… This keeps you prompt and not having to go back and touch something a second time.

> Mike Martone, Senior Regional Manager
> Cumberland Farms

For my work/life to be balanced I must take time in the morning to pray, exercise and eat a healthy breakfast. Then, no matter what happens the rest of the day, I am ready to take the time to listen, evaluate the situation and take the necessary action. I try not to handle a piece of paper more than once. I also try to respond to email and keep my inbox cleaned out.

> Mary Kay Vrba, Director
> Dutchess County Tourism

I put events or something I have to do into the calendar on my iPhone with an alarm; even if it's going to the gym, so they are not forgotten about.

> Erica Brandler CSW, CSS, Barefoot Wine & Bubbly
> Brand Development Manager
> Northern Area

My biggest time management tool is my electronic calendar. I have my whole life, both professional and personal on it. The biggest time management piece of that is to use the reminder function. That way, I receive a "heads up" that it is time to pay attention and look at my calendar to see what is on there.

Every Monday morning, the first thing I do is go through my entire week of calendar entries and make sure a reminder is set for each. That way, I am sure not to miss anything. Anything from a presentation to our CEO, to remembering to pick up my dry-cleaning on the promise date.

> John Holloran, Director, Sponsorship Marketing
> Global Headquarters
> Raytheon Company

As I manage up to forty people in different locations, I always ask when leaving me a phone message to include their question or request instead of just "please call me." It eliminates having to make a call to find out their reason for phoning while I'm able to work on their issue and reply to them once with an answer.

> Diane Rocco, Account Executive
> LVMH Fragrance Brands
> PARFUMS GIVENCHY * FENDI * KENZO PARFUMS * PUCCI

It's OK to have a "full in-box." It means people want to be engaged with you. They value you and your opinion. It's a great feeling.

> Judi Palmer, Director of Marketing and External Communication
> Stop & Shop/New England Division

I start each year by adding birthdays to the new calendar. I find that calling friends and family on their birthdays versus an email or Facebook shoutout, is a more personal touch.

> Michael Young, President
> Vision Marketing

Your Someday is Now.

We all know that a To Do list is an essential tool. I spend 10 minutes every single night organizing my To-List for the next day. However, I have found that having two separate to-do lists – my "Daily To-Do List" and a "Hope To-Do List" is the most effective way for me to manage my work and home life. I use Evernote and sync it on my work iPhone, personal blackberry, iPad and PC so no matter where I am, my lists are up to date and I can check off my tasks in real-time as I complete them. I also only write down (or type) the tasks that I realistically foresee that I can accomplish throughout the day on my "Daily To-List" listing the priorities (projects on deadline, meeting preparation, presentations, etc.) I DO NOT use this list for all the things that I hope to get done in the day, as I did in the beginning of my professional career. Instead I list these tasks or "To-Do's" on my "Hope To –Do List."

Nina Walsh, Social Media/Digital Marketing Strategist
UMass Memorial Medical Center

I rely greatly on my Franklin Covey planner to help keep me organized. I know a lot of people are using their iPhones and smart phones these days for organization. Maybe I'll get there some day, but for me, I like to be able to hold the book in my hands, as well as flip through the pages and calendars. Plus, you can store each year in a big binder. That way, if you ever need to refer back to a date or you're looking for contact information, it's all right there.

Mike Fraioli, Brewery Representative, RI
Harpoon

In the last year, I started placing calendar appointments with the most important tasks I need to accomplish each week. Generally, I have a few one-hour appointments with myself each week to be sure I accomplish each big task before answering email just eats up all my time.

John Henley, Chief Operating Officer
Center for Sales Strategy

When reading email - do it, delete it or delegate it. Always trying to keep an empty in box.

Beth Steucck, CEO
New England Inns & Resorts

To avoid phone tag: When leaving a voicemail message, always leave a time or time frame for the best time you can be reached in addition to a phone number.

> Joe Rocco, President
> RocJo Productions

I set aside time each day to address email versus all day - once in the morning, once before lunch and once prior to finishing the day. If I read and try to respond to all emails as they come in, I tend to forget responding to emails.

> Rich Schuttenhelm, VP, National Accounts
> Dr Pepper Snapple Group

Answer your own phone, emails, letters, etc. Don't screen calls and if you have an organization, don't let anyone else have their calls screened. It's quicker, easier, cheaper, and satisfies your customers much more timely - regardless of what you say and keeps you focused. In the long run, it saves everyone the most TIME.

> NIROPE, Nick, Ron and Pete Cardi
> Cardis Furniture

Technology is incredible and has made all of our lives more productive in endless ways but the accessibility needs to be regulated. Look around in a meeting- how many phones are out and how often does the meeting get derailed because someone needs to take a call, respond to a text, or email? For those of us who started their careers when a facsimile machine was progressive, it is our responsibility to show the digital generation who knows no other way that listening and actually looking up and having a live interaction that is not on "the cloud," has become a lost art. Do what you can within your own circles to bring back meaningful communication.

> Michele Maker Palmieri, General Manager
> Newport Yachting Center

Two dings and a ring! When emails are not getting the point across and two emails have been exchanged, pick up the phone and give a ring.

> Carolynn Woodis, Training Specialist
> Amica Mutual Insurance

Chapter 8: Packrats and Productivity
Get Organized

Your Someday is Now.

"A place for everything and everything in its place."
-*Isabella Mary Beeton*
The book of Household Management, 1861

"Organization" has a different meaning for each of us. Some people prefer a clear desk or work space, while others prefer working on several accounts or projects at once, reflected by file folders and paperwork on their desk. A clean desk is not a manifestation of organization, just as a cluttered workspace does not mean you are unorganized. It is your choice to determine the style that works best for you.

Pack Rat

There are many reasons we save. One of the common reasons is that of nostalgia. We collect memories of good times and experiences – a child's art work, vacation souvenirs, thank you letters, Christmas card photos – the list goes on. Another reason we save is the anxiety of requiring the item in the future. My *Babciu* (Polish for grandmother) professed that we would have a future need for anything we threw away. She advised us to save *everything*. Her kitchen counter, bureau, car, and home were a testament to this philosophy. They were cluttered with items that were fascinating to me as a young child - jewelry, religious memorabilia, letters, papers and other bits and pieces.

Take a look at your life. As you observe your office, your home, your car, your garage, attic and basement, are there any improvements you can make? If you are comfortable with your clutter, embrace it. If you would like to clear up the clutter, let me offer a few suggestions.

Create an Organizational Plan or Checklist

Once you have made the decision to get organized, your plan or checklist can be as simple as listing or sketching the vision you have for your life, home, car, or desk. The first step with change or adjustment is the vision.

Schedule a Start and Finish Date

As you schedule a start and finish date, rest assured that you can always adjust the completion date. The important thing is to start. Therefore, schedule the day you will begin and the date you would prefer to have the project or task completed.

Focus on One Area at a Time

The thought of organizing can be overwhelming. Start with the books and magazines by the side of your bed, a kitchen drawer, a linen closet, the glove compartment of your car, or an area of your desk. When you organize one area that you are in contact with every day, it will give you the motivation to continue to clean and organize another space, and then another. It becomes a positive routine.

Make a Check List

Checklists offer an effective organizational tool. You can make checklists for packing, work, grocery shopping, doctor's appointments, your weekend "to do" list, and more.

You can also consolidate tasks to accomplish more. Make lists of what you have to do. Think in blocks of time –what can you accomplish in five minutes, fifteen, a half hour? What kinds of chores or tasks can you get done in the time allotted? My friend and former eighth grade teacher, Sister Theresita Donach, manages her "piles of paper" by working in fifteen or thirty minute blocks of time. She sets a timer and focuses on one or two tasks; for example - clearing her desk, filing paperwork, and discarding unnecessary documents.

Maintaining a tidy environment, whether it is your bathroom sink, kitchen counter, or desk can be a powerful time saver. Keep the "tools" you use in one place whether it is on your desk, in your kitchen, or another area. It will save you time in searching for them. Think about how your dentist, hair dresser, and mechanic keep all their tools at their fingertips, in one place.

Consolidate chores – put dishes directly into the dishwasher instead of letting them pile up in the sink. Plan one or two days a week to attack your laundry pile. Transfer clothes from the washing machine to the dryer in a timely manner to avoid cleaning them twice. Hang up items of clothing that do not require ironing so they do not sit in a dryer for hours. Wash and dry your socks in a mesh bag to avoid "missing sock syndrome." Purchase the same style and color of socks for your children as this will assist with matching the socks that you do find!

Keep your keys in the same location – at home and at work. At home, you can keep your keys in a drawer or on a special hook. At the office, keep the keys in your purse, jacket pocket, or by the door so you do not inadvertently lock yourself out.

Powerful Time Saving Tactic Checklist:

✓ Arrange items in an orderly manner.
✓ Switch dishes to dishwasher while talking on the phone.
✓ Change clothes from washer to dryer in a timely
  fashion to avoid washing again.
✓ Store your "tools" in one place.
✓ Keep your keys in the same location.
✓ Purchase the same color and style of socks!

Your Desk

When it comes to your desk, practice efficiency. Keep the items that you use everyday in close range. Whether it is your stapler, tape, phone, or files – place them where you can find them in a "5 second test."

If you are a visual person and like to display your files to keep them top of mind, consider storing them on a file rack on your desk or credenza. If you would prefer a clear business area, put your files away. Paperwork is overwhelming. When you are not able to maintain electronic files, create tangible paper file folders that work best for you. For instance, create "To be filed," "Just do it," "Action," or "Clip and read" folders for articles or paperwork that you would like to "clip" and read at another time.

Efficiency – Your Desk Checklist:

✓ Do I use it everyday?
✓ "To be filed" folder.
✓ "To do TODAY" folder.
✓ "To do" or "Action" folder.
✓ "Clip and read" folder.

Templates

Documents that you repeatedly use such as letters, invoices, reports, agreements, and meeting agendas should be created in templates that are easily accessible. This will save a great deal of time so that you are not creating forms or correspondence from scratch every time you require them.

Efficiency – Templates:

✓ Frequently used letter (thank you, project, introductory).
✓ Invoices.
✓ Contracts, proposals, reports.
✓ Meeting agenda and meeting minutes.
✓ Computer procedures and best practices.
✓ Timesheets.
✓ ??? Customize a template that works for you.

Time Sheets – Focus on Productivity

While I am not necessarily a proponent of timesheets, being required to use them for close to two decades assisted me in monitoring my time, thus gaining an understanding of how my hours at work were being spent.

If you find yourself a bit unfocused or distracted during the day, use a timesheet and a "To Do" list to get yourself focused on productivity. You are only misleading yourself if you are unproductive. It will lead to longer days, nights and wasted time.

Efficiency and Accomplishment

Entering the workforce in the 80's, I was taught that the best and most loyal employees worked 60 to 80 hour weeks. And, I worked them! Being seen at the office after 5:00 p.m. or on weekends was a visual demonstration of loyalty.

Flash forward to the 21st century and the focus is on efficiency. While there are some companies that may still measure an employee by the hours that are worked, most companies are interested in what is *accomplished* within those hours.

In working those long hours, I missed out on many family and friend activities. More times than I want to admit, my day would "kick in" at 5:00 p.m. as there was peace and quiet in the office, with the exception of others who also worked late. I was not effective working that many hours.

Without balance, you burn out. You get bitter, slam file drawers, and lose your motivation. You may start bullying others in addition to judging their projects or the way they spend *their* time at work.

Technology has created the 24 hour, 7 day a week business world. It is our responsibility to utilize this opportunity on our own time line, and additionally, learn how to relax and recharge.

There will always be a "busy season" in addition to periods of growth, budgeting and product launches that will require working overtime. However, to be at work for "appearances" or to "see and be seen" is a waste of time and productivity.

Your results and effectiveness speak louder than the extensive hours you work. In sales, marketing, business, or technology, there will always be *another* great idea, *another* client to entertain, *another* networking event to attend. Your goal should be maximum performance – personal and professional.

When you identify best practices in your personal and professional time management and create efficiency templates, you can accomplish a great deal in an eight hour day. You are worth much more than the hours that you work, providing you are "present" in your job and of course, "All in!"

Your Someday is Now.

What Are You Waiting For?

I have a new time management/organizational technique that I am using. I was finding that I constantly had piles of paper on my desk (not good-I need a neat desk). So now I have a different colored folder for each day of the week that I put paper work in based on the day I plan to work on it. Keeps me organized; hides the paper I'm not working on; I don't feel as overwhelmed by the sight of unorganized piles of paper and makes for a much more visually appealing desk.

Vince Burks, Senior Assistant Vice President and Communications Director
Amica Mutual Insurance Company
Corporate Communications Department

My tip is not all that life changing, by any means. However it is a tip that I recently took from a friend of mine. I purchased clear plastic containers and have organized all of my shoes – each pair in a different container and a 'post it' inside facing out with a quick description of the shoe (i.e., black suede flat, burgundy heel, etc.); no more shoe boxes of varying sizes. I love the way my closet looks. My friend is the Rhode Island Imelda Marcos and her shoe closets (yes plural shoe closets) look great!

Kathleen A. Charbonneau, Vice President, Community Relations
BankNewport

Most of my time is spent writing emails, and typically a number of my emails are similar – declining an event, requesting a media promotion, etc. Thus, I have a collection of typical emails already written up and saved on a document so that I do not have to spend time thinking through the best way to craft my words.

Brooke Rodriguez, Marketing
Southwest Airlines

Handle each piece of paper only once, then file it. Do not keep moving it from pile to pile.

Lisa Pratt, VP, Human Resources
Memorial Hospital of RI

Both personally and professionally, leave toiletries in one small bag. This bag is always ready which is especially helpful in an emergency.

Additionally, identify your key items, for instance, chapstick, hand lotion or sanitizer and stash all over the place – in your purse, car, drawer and couch. This way, they are always at your fingertips.

> Amy Murphy St-Laurent, Director of Marketing and External Communication NYC
> Stop & Shop Supermarket Co

The only way I can manage my professional time properly is by handwriting in my Day Timer Planner. I list my projects and appointments daily, prioritize them by letters and numbers (i.e A1 is a top priority), check them off as they are accomplished or completed, or move them to the next or another day. I learned this several years ago by taking a Franklin Covey class which instantly changed the way I managed my time. I used to write things down on a pad but this is so much more effective. I save one year's worth and refer back to it if I need the communication to revisit matters.

> Dave Izzo, Senior Account Executive
> Palermo's Pizza

I pad my schedule. If I have three calls and I think one will be about 40 minutes, I schedule an hour for it. If I think it's going to take 20 minutes to get somewhere, I schedule 30, etc. This way, either I have a little breathing room to get oriented for the next call or I'm not stressed out when unexpected things come up or things take longer than I thought.

> Sharon Hoyle Weber, Speaker/Author
> *Hot in the Pot, A Survival Guide for the Real You in the Corporate World*

Your Someday is Now.

Chapter 9: "On the Road Again"
Travel Efficiency and Effectiveness

Your Someday is Now.

"Like all great travelers, I have seen more than I remember and remember more than I have seen."

-Benjamin Disraeli

Ah travel! Travel offers us so much knowledge, opportunity and excitement. It can also be overwhelming and aggravating. While we do not have control over delays, weather, or other factors, we do have control over what we *do* during the time we spend travelling.

Plan for Delays

As we reviewed, there will be times that you are left waiting at a doctor's appointment, Department of Motor Vehicles, an oil change, or business appointment. Bring items with you – magazines, articles downloaded on your smartphone or tablet, cards to write to friends, or a book to read so you are using this time efficiently.

You may also face delays when traveling. You cannot change a delay at the airport, bus, or train station. However, if you prepare accordingly, you can benefit from travel time and unexpected delays by reading a book, answering your email, or enjoying a cup of coffee with a new friend or friends and colleagues you are traveling with.

Prepare travel files and carry them with you. What these files are comprised of is up to you - thank you notes to write, spread sheets to review, or newsletters to catch up on. When you use your travel and solitary time efficiently, it will give you more time when you are home so you can be *present* with the friends and family who matter most.

Pockets of Time

If you are in search of professional and personal growth – read and listen to uplifting or spiritual articles and books. You may want to learn more about time management, leadership, sales, social media, business, or customer service. You may want to use your time to read books on fly fishing, gardening, cooking or travel.

There are many ways to utilize brief pockets of time for your own personal self-development. Do you want to learn a language, read more books, take a course at a university, improve your golf swing, read an entire newspaper?

Whether you drive 5 minutes or 5 hours, use your car as an opportunity to increase your knowledge. I have heard this referred to as "Automobile University." Listen to business, education, and motivational CD's and load your iPod, iPad, MP3 player or smartphone with podcasts and audio books that interest you. You can learn a new language or listen to a new bestseller. Take time to discover radio stations that you enjoy for the music or educational content. You may start looking forward to long car rides! This opportunity to listen and learn can also be applied at the gym, cleaning your house or while taking a walk – exercise your body *and* your mind.

Whatever it is, discover these pockets of time and use them for YOU!

The Tank is Half Full

When we were growing up, one of our family "rules" and courtesies was to ensure that the gas tank in the cars that we shared was always half full – especially in the winter.

It takes one incident of running out of gas to realize that a full gas tank will reduce stress and improve your productivity, in addition to offering peace of mind. Keep your gas tank above half at all times.

Are there other things in your life can you leave stocked or half full? Consider your refrigerator, toiletries, and office items.

Your Packing Checklist

Packing can be stressful. When we were younger, my mother always had us create a packing check list. You can minimize "packing panic" by creating travel packing check lists and storing them where you can find them. Before the days of smartphones, I stored the lists in my suitcases – making copies of personal and professional packing lists and storing them in each suitcase so they were right at my finger tips. Store your lists electronically or printed out, whatever works best for you. If you travel a great deal, keep one suitcase packed and ready to go with toiletries, gym clothes, pajamas, etc…Purchase duplicates to ensure your bags are always packed with items that you use on a daily basis (shampoo, make-up, toothbrush, deodorant, smartphone chargers, etc…)

Where's My Charger?

We can always improve our personal efficiency. Among the most frequently forgotten items in hotel rooms are computer, tablet, and smartphone chargers. Keep your charger in the same location every time you travel – by the side of the bed, on the desk, or in the bathroom. This way you will always remember to pack it when you depart. Other common items left behind en route to a business or vacation trip include a toothbrush and deodorant. Yikes!

Here's Looking at You, Kid

There is no downside to looking great when you travel, especially by air, as you never know who you will meet.

There is an advantage to wearing the appropriate attire while you travel. If your checked luggage does not arrive, you will have a suitable business or vacation outfit. Additionally, while mid air or waiting to board, you may meet a potential client or new friend.

Plan your travel wardrobe in accordance with the four seasons or two seasons, depending on the climate where you live. Choose four clean and neat outfits to be your "go to" ensemble for travel. Make sure the clothes are comfortable, wrinkle free, and that the shoes you wear come off easily at the security check point.

Pack your carry-on bag with your essentials – medicine, personal hygiene items, and an extra set of clothing or two. You will be well prepared if your luggage gets lost.

Chances are, when you are prepared, your luggage *will* arrive to your destination.

Where Do *Your* Keys Live?

True story. On the last leg of a flight after being away from my family for several days, I boarded the airplane with my purse and one carry-on item – a small computer bag. Due to space on this particular plane, they asked me to check the small bag as I entered the jet way.

I removed my laptop from the bag and placed it in my purse. The flight attendant took the bag to store with the other checked luggage. As the plane took off, I realized the keys to my car and house were in the bag she had just checked and I would be landing well after midnight. The short flight appeared particularly long as I worried about the keys in my checked bag. I was concerned that my bag would not be stowed with the other luggage when they took it from me.

When we landed, my luggage (complete with computer bag) arrived safely at baggage claim. Whew! Lesson learned – keep your keys in the purse, briefcase or small carry-on that is *guaranteed* to accompany you.

That's where my keys live.

Go Away – Relax, Recharge, Renew

It is very important to schedule time off to recharge. This is time that will renew your energy and enthusiasm for work.

Vacations are important. You work hard and whether you take a long weekend, one week or two weeks to enjoy time off, make sure you spend time doing what *you* want to do.

Perhaps reading a book every day relaxes you. Maybe you want to watch back to back episodes of *Law and Order* or *Downton Abbey*, your favorite sitcom, or a movie marathon. You may want to use your time off to learn a new skill – cooking, scuba diving, tennis, skiing, surfing, or sailing. Take a week or long weekend and immerse yourself in an activity that appeals to you.

Vacation Tips:

Turn Off Your Smartphone!

You will truly relax when you shut off and store your mobile phone, Droid, iPhone, iPad, or Blackberry. Many executives will argue that this is not possible: *"Do you know how important I am, Gail?"*

It seems, however, that we are *all* very important. If you look around a restaurant, you will see families individually occupied on phones and gaming devices. Often they hold the phones while eating! What is "so important" that an eight- year-old cannot shut off his or her phone or put a handheld video game away during dinner?

You will enjoy more quality time with your friends and family when you shut off contact to the outside world to be *fully present* with the people you are with.

Mini Breaks - Relax and Recharge

You've worked hard. Take time to play 18 holes of golf or go away for a ski weekend. Take a day to visit a spa. Enjoy a massage, pamper yourself with a pedicure and then make use of the sauna, hot tub, and relaxation room.

Many people feel guilty taking vacation time away from work. In fact, some people will wear not taking vacation time as a badge of honor.

My mother and father both worked very hard. That said, they always scheduled time for family vacations, whether it was a week away with International Weekends, a week in Williamsburg, or several long weekends each year. We also enjoyed summers in Rhode Island with books, board games and three television channels. Our summers were full of outdoor activities – swimming, water skiing, jogging, baseball games, and bike riding.

Vacations need to be planned and it gets harder to schedule the time as you get closer to the date and have yet to make accommodations or airline reservations. Your vacation time is a component of your compensation. Unless you are getting paid cash for the vacation days you do not take, you are paying your company a week or two of your salary when you forfeit vacation time.

And unless finances are very tight, the currency of time spent with friends and family or simply to recharge, outweighs financial remuneration for time at work *versus* time for you.

Your Someday is Now.

Do Something Different- Volunteer or "Voluntour"

"Never doubt that a group of thoughtful, committed citizens can change the world. Indeed, it is the only thing that ever has."

- Margaret Mead

My father, Dr. Jeremiah Lowney, founded the Haitian Health Foundation (HHF) in the early 1980's. His initial voyage to Haiti was in February, 1982. He was accompanied by my brother Mark, then a student at Boston College. What was astounding is that my father had just been operated on for cancer in the fall of 1981 after being told by several doctors that he had one year to live. My father will tell you (with great appreciation followed by a wink), that 30 years later, he has been blessed with a very "long year!"

During his first years in Haiti, in the slums of Port-au-Prince, my father became friendly with the Missionaries of Charity, an order of sisters founded by Mother Teresa of Calcutta. At the request of Mother Teresa, he went on to establish an unparalleled nonprofit organization in the rural, southwestern city of Jeremie, Haiti. With a dedicated HHF-salaried, Haitian staff, the public health program umbrella has matured from initially serving 38,000 people in 25 rural villages to now covering over 230,000 people in 104 villages. HHF's outreach has always focused on the most vulnerable – women, children and the elderly.

In 1983, during my junior year at Tufts University, I had the privilege of visiting Haiti for the first time, on a medical mission with my father. This life-altering experience prompted me to create a course for the Experimental College at Tufts University entitled: *Ever Compete With A Pig? Making It In The Third World*. To witness people and pigs competing for food on a garbage dump, as if this was a natural way of life, was a complete shock and truly a "wake up call."

For over three decades, I have had the privilege of volunteering and fundraising for the poor of Haiti. Involvement with HHF has been an *opportunity* versus *obligation* for me, my siblings and friends.

While I think about Haiti every single day and do my best to fundraise for HHF year round, volunteering in Haiti for a week each year recharges me. With every visit, one gains a new appreciation for the most basic things in their lives – food, a table to put it on, running water, healthcare access, a bed, a clean bathroom - or a bathroom in general, for that matter.

It is encouraging and inspiring to see, first hand, the tremendous improvements that have been made by HHF for the people of Haiti.

My sister, Marilyn Lowney, is the Executive Director of HHF. She works with my father and mother (two unpaid volunteers) to raise the dollars and resources required to keep the clinic and outposts not only funded, but running smoothly. She is an "ambassador of good will," serving the poorest of the poor with an inspiring energy level and great deal of patience. Whether she is writing grants or organizing projects (health care, education, nutrition, or housing), she does not waste a minute; her time management is stellar. Additionally, she also has a very special way about her with both the Haitian people we serve and the volunteers who visit with us for a week or years.

Looking Beyond Yourself

Choosing to use your vacation time to help others will benefit *you* even more than the people you are helping. Whether you choose to assist in the United States or internationally, "voluntourism," is a different way to enjoy and explore during your vacation, offering a rich and rewarding experience.

To look beyond ourselves and make an impact on this world, no matter how large or small, is a gift we give ourselves.

I am convinced that the happiest people are those who in some manner serve others without any desire for recognition or personal gain.

Be Where You Are

Several years ago, a friend asked me, *"When you travel for business or to Haiti, don't you miss your family?"* Of course I do, but I also believe it is important to *be* where you are. There is no sense in pining or longing to be in another location. Put your energy into what you are doing, the people you are with and the tasks at hand. When you are with your family, the same applies. Put down the technology and be present. The gift of time together, is the greatest gift of all. *Be* where you are.

Vacation and Leisure Activities

Planning Work Sheet

List four activities you would like to do over the next six months (i.e. Commence a fitness routine, take tennis lessons, visit with a friend once a week, volunteer at a non profit organization, take yoga classes, run a 5K, etc...).

1)

2)

3)

4)

List four weekend "get-aways" or "stay-cations" –

Plan one for each quarter – spring, summer, autumn and winter (i.e. City weekend with theatre and fine dining, cozy visit to a B&B, ski weekend, spa weekend, volunteer or educational weekend).

1)

2)

3)

4)

List a vacation that you would like to take this year – (i.e. The location, length of time, and the activities you would like to participate in).

Your Someday is Now.

What Are You Waiting For?

My life is sort of like George Clooney in the movie, *Up in the Air*, but not that bad, thank goodness. However, I had to chuckle at the way he packed and went through security checkpoint at airports. He had it down to a science.

My business trips are typically for 3-4 days each week. I plan out my outfits ahead of time for business meetings and any after hours fun. A pair of jeans and a pair business pants save room in my one carry-on bag. I pack one pair of shoes that can be worn day or night. I also leave room for running shoes and workout gear because it's easy to let yourself go when traveling. I also pack a pair of socks to walk around in the hotel room because no matter how many times they vacuum, it's never perfectly clean.

For frequent travelers, pick an airline (like Southwest) and hotel chain for points. They add up fast. After a few trips, you too will get a routine and move through airports like a pro! Safe travels!

> Steve Sisneros, Director of Airport Affairs
> Southwest Airlines

When traveling: roll your clothes instead of folding them in your suitcase. You can fit a lot more in and they seem to come out less wrinkled.

> Sheryl Spanos, Entrepreneur
> Portsmouth, RI

Business travel is the most difficult component, as it takes you away from home and family. It is important to remain in communication, and never forget what you are doing all the hard work for. Most critical, is to be sure to give your full attention. At work, be at work; with family, be fully with family. As they say, it is the quality, not the quantity of what you give that matters.

> Luke Sessa, VP, Private Brands
> HH Brown Inc

I've made it a practice to NEVER work on airplane trips.

When I have to travel far or quasi-far distances for work – I pretend those hours are a bonus gift for me. To actually have enough time to read a novel or really crap magazines, to have a cocktail (I am a woman who knows how to say hello to an early Bloody Mary with gusto!) or attack a book of New York Times crossword puzzles. Mostly, because embracing my very rare moments alone and letting my brain decompress and kick-back – makes me a better boss, businesswoman, and mom – and also because GOD forbid anything ever happen on my flight and the last thing I was doing was work!

Seriously – I so rarely get to daydream without an email, text or loving elbow tug interruption – that when I do – and I allow myself to go with it. I find I am more creative and mentally refreshed – even if my neck hurts and my legs are sort of cramped. Final tip — pack quality snacks!

Margie Fox, President and Founder
Maloney and Fox

As I travel a great deal, I am about speed and not leaving items behind.

This may be easier for guys, but I always wear some kind of jacket on a trip. When I approach security, my watch, wallet, and anything in my pockets are in my jacket and I remove it to place in the bin with my small plastic bag of liquids, shoes and belt....4 items.

I also now carry an iPad instead of a laptop. As iPads do not need to be removed from your carry-on, you only use one bin.

Speaking of carry-on....I never check a bag as this saves time on both ends of the trip. I always place my bags in front of my bin so that when they come through, my roller bag is open and ready for my toiletry bag when it comes through the bin. My shoes are thrown on the floor (try to wear slip on shoes) and I am getting back in my shoes while I am putting on my jacket. I am then ready to walk away from the area with only my belt in hand to finish... I get through fairly quickly and back "dressed," ready to go.

Gary Stiffler, CEO/President
The Matlet Group

Your Someday is Now.

As I travel often, I have thorough standard packing checklists for each kind of domestic or international travel I am going on: work, pleasure, and especially more unique trips like volunteering in Haiti with the Haitian Health Foundation. These core lists ensure I won't forget any necessities such as extra contact lenses, various chargers, or foreign electric plug adapters for when traveling overseas, etc.

This simple thing saves me time on going through mental checklists before each trip and alleviates unnecessary anxiety.

Colleen Hopkins, President
Hopkins Events

I walk at airports wherever possible as this is a good way to get exercise. For example, at Denver or Atlanta airports, rather than taking the train, I walk between terminals. Also, when on a day flight, I avoid sleeping on the plane so that I am tired when I land and avoid jet lag as much as possible. Even when flying to Asia or back from Europe, I try to stay awake.

I never drink alcohol on a plane. On evening and night flights, I avoid eating.

A personal quirk is I only like flying airlines that have personal televisions, it is a great way to get caught up on movies and make time go by faster. I also would rather fly economy and stay at a 5 star hotel when I arrive than fly business and stay at a cheaper place.

Mark Glazier, Global Marketing/Business Development Executive
Calgary, AB, Canada

When packing for a long trip, bring all neutral colored clothing that create easy outfits that will cut down your packing time, morning preparation and luggage weight. Pack jeans, pants, sweaters and shirts all in basic colors that you can mix and match to create a multitude of ensembles. Bring printed scarves, patterned ties, statement jewelry, or colorful shoes that could be added to complete each look.

Allison Brickman, Partnership Sales Coordinator
Newport Harbor Corporation

Picture stress as little drops of water filling a bath tub. For a while they are very easily accommodated, but as the bathtub fills, those same size drops can cause overflow. When you go on vacation, you empty the tub. There is probably never going to be a time for you to go on vacation that works for the whole office. Some colleagues and clients may be annoyed when you are gone but you need to empty the tub so that you can once again handle the stress easily. Not only is vacation fun and good for you- it's good for them and your work too. So go out there and empty your bathtub!

Alyson Singer, Producer
Boston, MA

When I travel, I want to make sure I do something authentic. With business travel, you are darting to the hotel, meeting, airport. We need to take more away from a city than schedules and meetings. I try to find a great restaurant or site that the city is know for, in essence, walk "the beach" and find the "seashell" of the place.

Evan Smith, President
Discover Newport

I always retrieve my keys out of my coat pocket when hanging up or checking my coat in a public place. Good thing. Once I grabbed my keys first before hanging my leather jacket up in the foyer of the church hall where the community chorus I belonged to rehearsed. There are different support groups that meet in the upstairs on the same night so lots of people pass through the foyer. Three hours later, when I went to leave, my jacket was gone. Stolen from a church hall! At least I had my keys to drive home and get back into my apartment.

Janine Weisman, Editor
Mercury

Traveling back and forth to Haiti, it is important to maximize space in my suitcases for essential items. I use the vacuum bag system.... *Voila!* It becomes the magical Mary Poppins bag!

Marilyn Lowney, Executive Director
Haitian Health Foundation

I keep a Word document of all the toiletries that I need for travel and print it out for each trip. I also write the number of days I'm traveling and assign an outfit for each day to prevent over packing.

Tiffany Hodes Waddell, VP of Client Relations
NETC

My two strategies for fun, successful trips are to be patient and to keep my eyes wide open. Of course, patience is important for the obvious travel challenges like delayed flights and lost bags, but it's also vitally important in encountering new people, new places, and new cultures. I try to remind myself that just because I might be used to things happening a certain way, does not mean that is the only way. More often than not, keeping this in mind has resulted in learning new concepts and solutions, having great conversations with interesting people, and always, enjoying the journey! Also, sometimes when I'm riding through a new city I'll catch myself scrolling through emails or reading news on my phone, when I remind myself to snap out of it and take in the new surroundings. You never know where a great idea or inspiration might come from!

Anne Marie McLaughlin, Director of Marketing & Communications
International Tennis Hall of Fame & Museum

Under my bathroom sink, I keep several clear, stackable plastic containers, each stocked with travel size products. Kept with these containers is a small travel bag already organized with my necessary sundry items – shampoo, deodorant, sunscreen, hand sanitizer toothbrush, toothpaste, etc. This way, the bag is "suitcase ready," or at least, easily restocked. I also keep my carry-on travel ready by never unpacking it completely. It is always ready to go with a pair of warm comfy "travel" socks, pens, reading glasses, and a small bag with aspirin, band-aids, hand moisturizer, ear plugs and hand wipes. When it's time to go, all I need to add is my wallet and Kindle! I have found that by minimizing the time I use to pack the things that must ALWAYS go with me, I reduce my packing stress.

Robin Thayer Harmon
Harmon Recovery Foundation

Chapter 10: "Bless and Release"
These are *Your* Happy Days

Your Someday is Now.

"Enjoy every minute, live every heartbeat, these are your happy days."

- *Frances "Babciu" Winiarski*

I am the oldest of four children. On many evenings, around 5:00 p.m., our mother found herself exhausted by our energy levels. Four children under the age of 7 had unrelenting needs and demands. When she could no longer tolerate the commotion, she would proclaim, *"I, I, I," - it's not all about you. There are four of you!"*

My mother taught us the importance of looking beyond "I" (ourselves) and learning to be thoughtful of others. However, there are times when you should focus on yourself. As you get older, I prefer to call it "experienced," you learn a few secrets pertaining to balance.

When traveling by airplane, flight attendants offer instructions including, *"In the case of emergency, put the oxygen mask on your face before assisting the person next to you."*

As on that airplane, sometimes you need to put yourself first – more *"I, I, I"* in order to have the energy to bring *your* best to others. You need to add more "Recharge" time back into your life.

Stop running. Cultivate your inner calm. Make a list of peaceful thoughts. Enjoy candlelight, a cozy fireplace, and a warm bowl of soup. Take time to enjoy your friends, family, and time for you.

Seven "Recharge" Tips

- Make appointments with yourself.
- Block activities with your family as if they were meetings.
- Turn off your cell phone.
- Leave work at work.
- "Date" your spouse or partner.
- Capture your energy.
- Bless and release.

Let's review seven "Recharge" tips that will offer more time for you.

Seven "Recharge" Tips

1) Make Appointments with Yourself

Take time off to relax, read a book, go to a movie, or participate in an activity that you enjoy. Don't let anyone make you feel guilty for doing something for yourself - we all need time to revive! If you do not want to spend your personal time cleaning your house, hire a cleaning professional. (Note: One of my friends stopped purchasing coffee every morning and splits the "savings" between donations to non-profits and cleaning assistance twice a month.)

Add personal appointments to your calendar with the same importance as business appointments. This way, whether it is a bicycle ride, coffee with a friend, visit with a therapist, game of tennis, or attending your child's or friend's activity, it will really happen.

Once you write it down, chances are you will attend the engagement. If you need to change the appointment, immediately reschedule it.

If you appreciate beautiful nails, take the time to get a manicure. Give yourself permission to work in your garden instead of opening e-mail on a Sunday afternoon.

When I planned and produced weddings and corporate events, my work day seemed to start at 5:00 p.m., after working all day! I felt the energy "kick in;" the exodus of other employees offered a semblance of solitude. That's when I would complete paperwork and return phone calls. There are several businesses that are not "9-5" and the hospitality business is one of them.

These days, 5:00 P.M. has switched to 5:00 A.M.

I wake up early and the extra hour of "alone time" assists me with getting so much done - writing, exercise, email and household organization prior to departing for work.

There are also careers in the hospitality field, for instance; the sales, marketing and production of events or venue management, that require working nights and weekends. The summer is often the busy season. While friends and family are enjoying the summer, you are working for weeks and perhaps months at a time. It is difficult to establish balance and "find" time.

What time of day works best for you at this point in your life and how can you find pockets of time for YOU?

How can you work *smarter* within *fewer* hours?

2) Block Activities with Your Family as if They were Meetings

When you walk out of work at the end of your day, which may be at the height of other people's "busyness," simply say goodbye or *"Have a great night - see you tomorrow."*

Ignore comments and joking from co-workers, for instance, *"It must be nice to take time off for your son's baseball game." "Wow - you're taking Saturday off when we are all working?" "Gee, going out to lunch again? I don't have time to eat away from my desk."*

You do not have to offer excuses or a diatribe on where you are going. You will only aggravate people when they are still sitting there working. They may have arrived at work later than you, spent time on water cooler chitchat, or attended too many meetings.

We are *all* inundated with work, and it is not slowing down anytime soon.

Your "time off" is *your* time off. Block your after work activities with your friends and family, in pen. They are as important, if not more important, than the work you do. It is not the hours you work, it is what you accomplish within those hours. Focus on results.

Besides, YOU are more than your work.

3) Turn Off Your Cell Phone

Do you struggle with "turning it off," physically and mentally?

Let's use your smartphone as an example - why not turn it off (or be selective in regard to who you respond to) when you walk in the door of your home at the end of the day? The end of the day is your time. It is your time to exercise, cook and enjoy a delicious dinner, enjoy the company of your family and friends, or simply embrace your privacy. It is your time to read the newspaper, a book, or watch a movie. It is your time to organize your personal life.

I entered the working world in the mid 1980's, when we did not have wireless devices to respond to questions or requests around the clock. We did not have cell phones for immediate connection. Phone calls were usually made and returned during the business hours of 9:00 a.m. to 5:00 p.m., rarely in the evening or on weekends.

My colleagues walked out of the office at the end of the day, whatever that time was for them, and went home. Perhaps they brought a trade magazine to read or office files, but there were no laptops or cell phones to physically bring into the homestead.

Flash forward to the 21st century. When my son, Samuel, was seven years old, I was on the phone with a client in the early evening. I 'sshhed' him when he gestured that he needed to talk to me. When I hung up, he walked up to me and softly said, *"Mom, please don't ever 'sshh' me again, I am your most important client."*

My heart fell as I asked, *"Where did you hear that?"*

Sam's reply? *"I heard it on a television commercial - a mom said her children were her most important clients."*

I would never consider Sam a "client." He is, however, the most important person in my life, along with my husband and family.

Why bring so much work home? You don't bring your family to work.

My husband also asked me, in his very polite way, if I could finish my business and personal conversations outside of the house instead of walking into the house at the end of the day, on the cell phone, in full "work mode." He is usually home earlier than I am and is cooking or relaxing with Sam when I barge in, full steam ahead! I had not realized how disruptive this was to my family.

What is the outcome of entering our home at the end of the day without talking on the smartphone?

As I walk in the door exclaiming, *"Hello family!"* – I receive the warmest hug and welcome from Sam. That hug is the best feeling in the world. Talk about a welcome home!

4) Leave Work at Work

"That's great Gail, but my workload is overwhelming and I have to bring it home."

There will always be "infinite" work, especially in certain professions such as sales and business development.

You are the *only* one who can analyze your day. Take an honest look and assess why you are not able to get your work done. Are you spending too much time mired in email or wasting time in meetings that are just too long? Are you lingering after meetings for "chit chat" unrelated to work? Do you have a long commute? Have you learned how to delegate?

You are the only one who truly knows how you are filling your time. If you are completely overwhelmed, you may want to talk with your supervisor about balancing your projects or search for a new job so you do not lose so much of your precious personal time, paddling upstream, every day, 365 days a year.

5) Date Your Spouse or Partner

"Dating" your partner is crucial whether you have been together for one year or fifty. It is important to continue to recharge your relationship as it shifts and changes. We cannot take *anything* or *anyone* for granted. It is imperative to keep listening and caring about your spouse or partner.

Don't let your appearance or intellect wane. Stay interesting and stay interested. While you both have separate lives, you want to ensure that you still live your life as a team in a solid partnership.

One of my friends holds Friday night sacred as the "date night" with her partner. If the same night each week does not work for your lifestyle, choose one night each week or a few nights each month. Go to dinner, a movie, the theater, a sporting event, a concert or another activity that will enable you to spend time together, enjoying each other's company.

Plan family vacations - whether a beach vacation, educational voyage, camping trip, "staycation" (time at home) or ski trip, with phones off. Spending family time together is *invaluable.*

Block these dates ahead of time, so when other things arise, you are already booked.

I didn't always have this vacation mindset. When I was younger, I was under the impression everything would fall apart at work if I was not there. Ah, the hubris of youth. I soon came to the realization that I was only one spoke of a very large wheel.

Although there will *always* be work to do, and there is seldom an ideal time to take a vacation, everyone can find the time to take a well deserved break. In fact, it is imperative to rejuvenate, relax and re-group with friends and family.

6) Capture Your Energy

It is important to recognize when you are at your best and most energetic.

We all have different times of the day where we are most effective. Do you find yourself more energetic in the morning, afternoon, or evening? Perhaps your energy flows fluctuate.

In my earlier working years, I was full of energy from morning until night, mostly because I loved what I did. As I get older, I get tired – even when working on projects I love.

How do you know when you are most productive? You are the only one who can determine this. For some people, there's not a set time. We all have a time when we are most productive and it may not be the same every day.

Take it day by day. How well did you sleep the night before? Be aware of your high energy times. Sometimes high energy time is first thing in the morning – one cup of coffee and you are wide awake. Other people may be groggy in the morning and experience energy bursts in the afternoon.

Where does your energy come from? You will usually find that you have a great deal of energy to work on the assignments you enjoy, the ones you look forward to. You will find yourself in your *flow*. When you are in this state of mind, you enjoy the task, class, or project so much, you do not realize the amount of time you have spent on it. When you find yourself in a positive and constructive state of flow, take advantage of it and do as much as you can, personally or professionally. Use your high energy time for tasks that demand it. You can always make the beds and fold the laundry when you are running out of steam.

In regard to tasks you "do not" look forward to and feel your energy wane as you commence them, reward yourself as you make progress. Your reward may be a walk to the local coffee shop or simply stepping outside into the fresh air. It can be enjoying a quick video or phone call with a friend.

Just be mindful of the time you take for a quick "surf" on the internet or another distraction that could procrastinate your return to projects.

Make your choices wisely!

7) Bless and Release

Try to eliminate one time waster – an activity, person, or process – from your life each week!

Have you outgrown a board or committee that you are on? There are many ways you can assist a non-profit group beyond attending a meeting. You can donate items for their raffles or silent auctions, assist with one fundraiser each year, attend the event and bring other people with you or send a considerable donation!

With regard to relationships, you must do your best to avoid people who drain your energy. This is, quite simply, the last thing you need in your life. It will affect your productivity, energy level, confidence, and spirit.

Keep a "time sheet" or activity log for one or two weeks and record your accomplishments. What did you do differently that led to an increase or decrease in productivity? What time wasters have you eliminated? How was your energy level?

Are the people, events, or processes filling your time, *worth* your time? If not, bless and release.

These are Your Happy Days

My *Babciu* was a very kind, spiritual and resourceful woman who raised seven children by herself when her husband unexpectedly died at age forty. Her home was always warm and cozy with the smell of delicious Polish cooking. She would host summer "dance parties" for me and my cousins. Through the summer, we would swim at midnight in the light of the full moon and sleep outside on her porch under a mass of blankets with the scent of sweet pea flowers and salt air.

Babciu shared her spirituality whenever we were together. She had a wonderful disposition and taught us appreciation for everything – sunshine, church, rosary beads, rainy days, friendships, and family. Her mantra was, *"these are your happy days,"* repeated daily. Her wisdom was focused on enjoying every minute and living every heartbeat with the people that we love.

Yes, these indeed are our "Happy Days!"

Na zdrowie! (Cheers and God bless you in Polish)

Your Someday is Now.

What Are You Waiting For?

Yoga has changed my life. It clears my head and helps my body grow stronger physically and mentally. Yoga opens your heart and when you open your heart, you open your mind.

> Kathryn Farrington, Vice President Marketing
> Discover Newport

The best thing I can do for myself is to make time to walk on the beach. I start with a full mind and by the end of it, breathing the salt air and listening to the ocean as my music, I clear my head and am ready to take on the world!

> Kathryn Whitney Lucey, Photojournalist
> Newport, Rhode Island

"Crockpot."

> Janine Weisman, Editor
> Mercury

These are a few thoughts for real life as well as work life:

Don't live life in a bubble. Take chances, make mistakes, seize opportunities, explore passions, discover new ones, never be afraid to laugh at yourself and don't forget to smile! And one more - make friends with your creative team.

> Krista Bridges, Account Executive
> In Marketing Services

I work out in the middle of the day, which refreshes me and keeps my energy level high for the afternoon. It also blows off morning tension and helps me keep afternoons from getting too stressful.

> Dan DiPiro, Senior Copywriter
> Stonyfield Farms

In balancing family and work, I find it refreshing to have boundaries on my time and live in the moment as much as possible. When multitasking, it is difficult to give your full attention to either task - someone or something is getting short changed! So when I am home, my attention is on my daughter, not scrolling through my email. Since spending my time like this I find I am more productive and clear headed.

> Danielle Stead Mancuso, Media Relations Specialist
> Rhode Island School of Design

- Put down the work at 5pm. I promise it will be there for you bright and early the next morning. Corollary: Get it done the next morning!
- Keep a piece of paper and pencil on your night stand so that you can easily write down something you may remember in the night. Or, ask your iPhone4 to remind you! Take advantage of technology!
- Don't overdo it during the holidays. Have one bin of decorations, not 10!
- Use your household scanner and "hire" your 10 year old to scan bills, statement, policies, etc... so you can shred the originals. Leave them in a file on your desktop.

> Dr. Jennifer Lowney, Orthodontist/Mother of four
> Norwich, Connecticut

The best piece of advice I can give a young professional is to immediately find a personal athletic goal upon entering the workforce. Every day, I receive the response from coworkers, "I never have the time." However, what many do not realize is learning to make time for activities such as training for a marathon teach professionals very early on how to manage time effectively. Additionally, athletic training creates drive, dedication, and the ability to overcome setbacks, all core skills looked for in ideal job candidates. And finally, exercise increases personal energy levels, making it easier to get through the day on nothing more than a night's sleep.

Avoid one of the most common time management pitfalls of young professionals and pick an athletic goal to achieve. Whether it is a 5k, 10k, obstacle race, or your first marathon, find your goal, make it fun, and inspire others to do the same.

> Joseph DiMuccio, Division Analyst, Middle Market
> The Hartford Financial Services Group

Your Someday is Now.

Get up an hour earlier than needed. Breathe, stretch and exercise, for a minimum of 30 minutes! This will allow you to focus on yourself and your well being, rather than the tasks at hand for the day. Those tasks and more will be there everyday. You need to clear your mind and strengthen you body in order to face them and accomplish them successfully.

> Dawn M. Speros, Yacht Consultant - Newport
> Gowrie Group

- Give yourself a break. It's important to take a coffee break, give your eyes a rest from the computer screen or even go outside for some fresh air. Let your mind rejuvenate and you'll in turn accomplish more. Always build down-time in your schedule to relax or even have fun.
- Stressful day? Think to yourself, what's most important right now? I like to call it, "pinpoint and prioritize." (Somebody, write that down and patent it!)
- No matter how stressed out you get, always remember that this is all part of the ride. Focus on the journey, not the destination. Everything else will fall into place.

> Natalia Kuziw, Assistant Media Buyer
> Deutsch

My stress reducing technique is to do something I love everyday whether it is go for a long walk, yoga, read a book, or arts and crafts. I try to make sure that I fit at least a half an hour to an hour of "ME" time in a day. My favorite stress reliever is to go on sunrise walks on the Cliff Walk. Walking so early in the morning clears my head and keeps me sane especially in the peak of the season.

> Amanda Barker, Private Event Sales Assistant
> Newport Yachting Center

When you are skiing, sailing, and enjoying time with your friends and family, put your phone away, relax and be there.

> Stewart Silvestri, America's Cup Team Member
> Stars & Stripes. 1987

- When cooking: double the recipe, one to enjoy today and one to freeze for the future... a true two for one delight in about the same amount of time.
- Let the kids help with your work or home tasks. A little filing, sorting, calculating, and balancing a checkbook can go a long way in life's lessons, not to mention that you get an extra set of hands to help. Understanding the basics can set a solid foundation for the future of our kids.
- Always take time to turn around and see who's behind you that might need some help as you make your way up the ladder of life. Extending a hand down to help pull someone else up is the greatest gift.

> Sheryl Spanos, Entrepreneur
> Portsmouth, RI

Holiday suggestions/recommendations:

- If you bake a lot of cookies it's easier to make all the batters one day so the next day all you're doing is the actual baking.
- Take your Holiday picture in the summer when all the children are together. It's harder to do this when they are running in different directions with sports during November/December.
- Make labels to address your Holiday cards. Do this at a time of year when you are not pressed for time.
- Do Holiday shopping during the year as you see gifts your family and friends would appreciate.

> Mary Ellen Schuttenhelm, Domestic Goddess
> CEO of the Schuttenhelm Organization

Your Someday is Now.

Chapter 11: Your Personal Brand
You are Your Own HR and PR Department

Your Someday is Now.

"Leadership is doing what is right when no one is watching."
-George Van Valkenburg

YOU Work for YOU

When you work for a company, *work* for it. You do not want to be known as the person who saunters into the office, whittles away time on Facebook, Twitter or other social media sites, lingers around the water cooler, or otherwise wastes time. Be honest with yourself - are you doing the best you can do, or are you "on strike" at work?

What is your reputation? Be known for getting it done, the "go to/make it happen" person in your company, community, and industry. Do your best to communicate clearly, stay organized, and finish your projects on or ahead of schedule.

You are *your* company. There are many times that your personal reputation will reach people before they meet you. What is the "word on the street" about you? Is it positive, negative, or indifferent? It is never too early or too late in your career to establish solid relationships and build a foundation of effective and respected work habits.

Once the word is out about you and your talents, success, and accomplishments, the sky is the limit.

Your Personal Brand

When you are in the presence of extraordinary leadership, you will recognize it. You will feel encouraged and empowered; noting the absence of whispering, secrets, or internal sabotage.

As a leader and your own "brand ambassador," be conscious of your personal and professional interactions. Within the relationships you will cultivate, *everyone* counts or nobody counts. Continue to build your personal brand by surrounding yourself with positive people who are successful in their own right.

You can also learn a great deal from people who do *not* do the right thing. You can learn how "not to be" by observing their actions.

Perhaps it is a boss or colleague who is always irritated, duplicitous, or unscrupulous in business. Perhaps it is a co-worker who "steals" work time by updating Facebook, shows up to the office late, takes long lunches, or spends time on lengthy personal phone calls throughout the day.

Worry about you – you cannot change others. Be known for *your* integrity, hard work, and dedication.

When I was in college, one of my professors suggested keeping a journal of unprofessional behavior that we witnessed simply entitled: *How Not to Be.* Start a journal of best practices in both the work place and in life. Create your *own* world - make it a positive and productive one.

Internal Relationships

> *"Leaders do the right thing; managers focus on doing things right."*
> *- Warren Bennis*

Trust is not instant; it takes time. The people who most often see your "best self" in the workplace are your clients. It is our colleagues, who are with us throughout the day and in some cases over forty hours a week, who discern our true nature.

You may work with people who put their best self forward for the external customer and treat their internal customers (co-workers or colleagues) with disrespect. No matter what your position is in a company, you should not take any of your relationships for granted. There is no place in life for burning bridges; you never know when you may have to walk back over them.

You cannot be two different people. There is no "on stage" and "off stage" in the workplace. It is "show time" – all of the time.

Audition for your job every day by bringing your "best you" to the workplace.

When you become the boss, leadership comes with challenges. It is a natural instinct for people to be envious. You may have employees (especially if they were inherited versus chosen) who falter in their loyalty quotient from time to time. This is human nature and, in many cases, you will not be able to change the people who work on your team. You can, however, change *your* mindset from a "work for" to "work with" mentality. Teenagers who work in an ice cream store during the summer work *for* a manager. Your team is working *with* you to ensure the success of a department or project.

There are two types of leadership – personal and positional. Think of them in terms of the concept of "push-pull." In the case of positional leadership, you were made the boss and people *have* to answer to you. You, as a leader, are "pushed" upon them.

With personal leadership, people gravitate towards you – they want to work *with* you and *for* you. They feel appreciated and honored through your actions and words. You "pull" them towards you.

What kind of leader do you want to be?

Internal Challenges

When you work with people on a daily basis, disagreements and misunderstandings will occur. Address the acorn before it becomes an oak tree. Tackle the uncomfortable situation or problem that people tend to avoid.

Internal disagreements waste time. Challenges must be addressed and solved immediately or they will discourage and demotivate the other employees in the workplace. The more people involved, the more time wasted.

When aggravation festers in the workplace, it breeds an unhealthy environment. Be the "better" person – address and discuss the problem with your colleague and solve it respectfully. If this is not possible, get your human resources department involved. We are in the workplace to work – not to create our own version of "Peyton Place" or "The Office."

Kaizen

If you have too many things on your plate, realize that you are most fortunate to live a life with many goals that you want to accomplish. You may not have the time to do it all at the current moment. The things that are important in your life will change and you will have to eliminate certain activities to add more to your calendar.

You can do or be anything you set out to achieve. It is never too late to be who you might have been and reinvent yourself. My eighty-year-old friends constantly amaze me with their new skills, hobbies, passions, and enthusiasm. My mother-in-law, Ruth, greets each day with appreciation and zest. She dresses beautifully, maintains an immaculate home, has a very active social life, and prepares a gourmet meal for herself almost every night. She does not miss a Newport Polo game in the summer or the Newport International Oktoberfest in the fall and her passion for people and life is inspiring.

My aunt Terry Winiarski Merrill was married at age 71 and enjoyed life and travel with Captain Sidney Merrill for the eight and a half years of their marriage. Their vibrant social life included winters in Florida and ballroom dancing throughout the summer. Their energy level alone was impressive!

Are you still searching for your "calling" or purpose? Is there is a certain career or activity you are drawn to? Identify people who are already doing it well. Observe these people. What are they doing to move forward? What are they doing in order to get things done?

Stay current! Keep up with the news via television, newspaper, or computer. Knowledge is everywhere - absorb it. Become a lifelong learner. After all, commencement, usually equated with graduation, means "beginning." Listen to other people, pay attention to their stories, and learn from them – personally and professionally.

Airline captains have "check rides" twice a year. This does not question their capability; it assures they stay at peak form. Account representatives at pharmaceutical and IT companies go through weeks of training to stay current or learn about new products. Sales teams fortunate enough to have quarterly or annual training learn new skills and reinforce best practices.

Be open to new ideas and personal improvement. To increase your value and productivity, ask for feedback from your personal advisors – whether personal or professional. It is one thing to *learn* and quite the other to *implement* the best practices garnered from professional development.

"Kaizen" is a Japanese word for continuous improvement. What are you doing to improve yourself every day to avoid "resting on your laurels?"

The Importance of Loyalty

When you work for a company, be "all in."

When you work with a group of colleagues, make sure to champion your team – internally and externally. Is there really a mistake so grave that you have not also made or would not be capable of making?

There is an inherent value in failure. When we stumble and make errors, as serious as they may be, we grow. As the adage states, *"It is not in the falling down, it is in the staying down."*

We all know colleagues and clients who disparage their company, boss, or co-workers. Take a good look at the people that you work for and with. Identify their strengths and focus on the positive. If that is not possible and you are truly in a toxic work environment, meet with your Human Resources department or start looking for fulfilling work elsewhere.

When you interview for a new job, talk respectfully about your current or former boss. Be courteous when you talk about your current or former companies. If you have nothing agreeable to share, avoid the topic of that company. Prior to the interview, mentally identify things you have learned throughout your career that you can share in the interview to illustrate your personal growth and value. What do *you* have to offer?

You are your own Public Relations and Human Resources department. You are your own brand.

What is the word on the street about you?

Horse Sense by Elbert Hubbard

If you work for a man, in Heaven's name work for him. If he pays wages which supply you bread and butter, work for him, speak well of him, think well of him, stand by him, and stand by the institution he represents.

If put to the pinch, an ounce of loyalty is worth a pound of cleverness. If you must vilify, condemn, and eternally disparage, resign your position, and when you are outside, damn to your heart's content, but as long as you are a part of the institution, do not condemn it. If you do that, you are loosening the tendrils that are holding you to the institution, and at the first high wind that comes along, you will be uprooted and blown away, and will probably never know the reason why.

Your Someday is Now.

What Are You Waiting For?

- I'm a big believer in "random acts of kindness." Corny, but I think it does more for the giver than the recipient.
- Act like a Leader and people around you will follow you, regardless of your title.
- I have a process for evaluating a situation it is; "Remain Calm, Don't Speculate, Get Facts, Make a Decision, Move On."
- I have a corollary to "Always be the calmest person in the room," it's "Always be the grownup in the room."
- I only fight the battles I "need" to win, as compared to battles I "want" to win. It sometimes takes wisdom and thought to figure the difference.

> Robert A. DiMuccio, President
> Amica Mutual Insurance Company

MBWA (Management By Walking Around). You will know more by talking to people and as a result, you get a better idea of operations – how to do it and get involved. This applies to everything from government affairs to the ball park. Familiarity will always help you.

> Larry Cancro, Senior VP of Fenway Affairs
> Boston Red Sox

Stay up to date on news in your industry.

An important part of your personal brand is being able to socialize and network with others in your industry. Reading blogs, magazines and websites with news on your trade will allow you to contribute to conversations with coworkers or networking professionals, giving off an impression that you are "in-the-know."

> Jen Cingari, Publicist
> ESPN Films and Original Programming

Have serious fun. You need to take your work (and life) seriously. However, in order to do so, you do not have to become a boring, mundane, frowning robot. It is possible to be a smiling, humorous, light hearted individual and still do a great job at work (and life). So, be serious, but don't forget to have fun, you will enjoy life more, and have more friends... I promise.

Which brings me to...

Keep things in perspective! There are many people who work in fields where they deal with life and death every day. Nurses, doctors, firefighters, military men and women... just to name a few. These are professions where every day the work they do can affect whether another human lives or dies. There are many other people who work in business, sales, retail or hospitality, etcetera, where if a mistake is made, small or big, no one will die as a direct result. So keep things in perspective! This does not mean stop working towards excellence, but if something goes wrong, don't overreact... keep things in perspective.

And last...

Make time for exercise! You only get one body, taking meticulous care of yourself needs to be a priority. Physical activity is necessary for a happy, healthy, balanced life. Schedule a yoga class or time to jog, and leave work behind when it's time to take care of you. If that seems impossible, schedule "walking meetings" with your colleagues, it is possible to discuss big ideas while you're moving your feet!

> Blakeley Schmidt, Senior Analyst
> The Cadmus Group

Always be genuine and true to yourself. Be the same person with your colleagues and prospective clients as you are with your family and friends and you will be the winner.

> Nancy E. Andrade, Director of Private Event Sales
> Newport Restaurant Group & Newport Yachting Center

Your Someday is Now.

My best time management practice is to stay active and passionate while maintaining an overall sense of moderation.

1. Media Diet - I manage my media intake by exploring 5 articles/talks a day.
2. Social Diet - I connect my active lifestyle with my social life and my husband and I host dinner parties with people from all walks of life once a month.
3. Food Diet - Fruit and complex carbs in the morning and lean proteins in the evening. Of course, dark chocolate is always welcome.

> Danielle Fay, Art Director
> Sapient Nitro

Listen. Just like we listen in our personal lives as to "where to go next," we should listen in business. This means slowing down enough (at least occasionally--a few minutes everyday) to ask if you're making the best decisions. I find that I accomplish more after taking an occasional breather from the day's sometimes frantic pace. From there you can better organize the remainder of the day, week or entire project.

On a larger scale I know I could have advanced quicker in my career (the ultimate time management) if I had "listened" to the fact that it was time for a new career challenge. Often, we innately know when it's best to ask for advancement or seek out new challenges but instead we stay in our comfort zones.

If you're finding you have less energy when you're walking into work everyday, stop and ask yourself why. Then listen. It might mean that status quo is no longer working for you or your company.

> Donna Mac, President
> DMacVoice & Media

- Tell the important people in your life that you love them every day.
- A great way to live your life: Be in Gratitude.
- Don't take it personally. Don't get defensive.

> Judi Palmer, Director of Marketing and External Communication
> Stop & Shop/New England Division

I catch two people doing something right and make it a point, weekly, to tell them how much they are appreciated. I find that investing time in my team creates a great working environment.

> Jeffrey P. Gagnon, CPCU, Assistant Vice President, Training and Development
> Amica Mutual Insurance Company

On the topic of "putting the big rocks first" and life balance, I think back to a day when I came home from work frazzled. I was scurrying around the kitchen getting dinner ready, dealing with the dogs, and a million other tasks. My usually self-sufficient son was at the table doing his homework. He periodically called out to me, "Mom?" I didn't have time.

"Just a minute," I replied each time, and continued with what I was doing. Once more he called out "Mom?" and I admittedly had a little difficulty hiding my frustration. "What IS it, Evan?"

"Mom," he said, "I'm writing this paper about how you're my personal hero, and I need a good opening line."

Ugggh! Talk about an instant resetting of priorities!

> Michelle Davidson, Director of Human Resources
> 99 Restaurants

Look where you want to go, not where you are. This piece of worldly advice came from a very unlikely source, at an unlikely time and place. I was having difficulty with a trick while snowboarding. My friend said to me, "Stop looking at your feet, that's your problem. Look at the end of the rail. Always look where you want to go, not where you are!" While his advice was directly pertaining to snowboarding at that specific time and place, this has stayed with me and I apply it to all aspects of my life. Stop looking at and settling with where you are in your job or life. Look to where you want to go and strive to get there.

> Robert A. DiMuccio Jr., Sales Representative
> Smith Optics

Your Someday is Now.

We live in a world that seems increasingly angry and conflicted. I want to find the good in each person and to acknowledge, praise and appreciate that good in each person.

Evan Smith, President
Discover Newport

In today's business world I have adopted a frame of mind which I think my customers find refreshing; "Stop managing to the drop down menu."

As professionals in today's fast paced computerized world, we are forced to maximize efficiency by checking a box or selecting a pre-determined reason for a customer issue. This ultimately forces us to remove individuality from our customers and their particular issues. We have all called a company and been forced to utilize the pre-recorded voice prompts only to find that our reason for calling is not represented by the prompts. In frustration we start pressing "0" on our phone hoping for an actual human to pick-up; a futile attempt at best. Remove this obstacle for your customers.

To be truly successful today, we must beat this system. Step outside and be EASY TO DO BUSINESS WITH to truly win your customer's business and loyalty. Select "other" from that drop down menu and treat your customers like the individual people they are. Be easy to work with and watch your business soar.

Thomas Riel, Senior Account Executive
Marriott International

There are so many variables in the world that affect us both personally and professionally, but your personal brand is something you can actually control. It all starts with some self-awareness and dedicated time to develop your brand mantra. After all, you are worth it. You represent the best brand in the world – YOU!

Rebecca Knapp LeBlanc, Senior Partnership Manager
Newport Harbor Corporation

People only see what you show them.

My mantra, something taught to me at a very young age by my mentor Benno Wissing (one of the top designers in Europe in the 70's) is "people only see what you show them." Sounds obvious, but so many people forget this and then are disappointed with how their clients or prospective customers react to presentations or projects that have left too much to the imagination. Step back from your projects/presentations before you present to your client/customer and look at it from their perspective. Make sure that what you are presenting as closely represents your thoughts and ideas for the solution to their problem and that you aren't depending on their imagination to understand what your solution is. First reactions are everything in presentation. You want to "wow" your client, not explain to them all of the stuff you are going to do, but is not evident in what you are presenting.

> Kathleen Kits van Heyningen, Senior Director- Creative & Customer Experience
> KVH

They call it work for a reason. It's not easy, but if you approach it with a positive attitude, you can have fun doing it. Work harder than anybody. You can have a lot of talent, but if you don't put forth the effort, talent docsn't amount to anything.

> Wayne Charness, Senior Vice President, Global Communications
> Hasbro

1. Life is Business and Business is Life
2. Sales is Everything and Everything is Sales
3. Everything is Cost vs. Benefit (so always add value)
4. Problem Solving is Key….ANALYZE
5. No Experience is Wasted….OBSERVE
6. Succeed- Do not envision another result
7. Internal and External Customers are everywhere and equally important

> Brian Cotsonas, Eastern Regional Sales Manager
> Smith Optics

Your Someday is Now.

I believe it is important to have multiple generations in the workplace. The younger generation can help the older generation with their technological struggles and the older generations can give the younger all the knowledge they have from experience. If we give each other advice on the areas where we need help, in the end we will all become better employees. It's always good to look at something from a different angle; working with different generations will help us all to do this.

TJ Donovan, Corporate Partnerships Event & Operations Coordinator
Newport Harbor Corporation

I believe that how you are dressed and groomed make a big impact on how you are perceived by others. I know there are days when I am getting dressed before work and all I want is to be comfortable. Then I will stop and think about who I might see at the restaurant that day/evening. I always want to be sure I am offering the best impression I can of myself and the people and restaurant that I represent. It makes me more confident and it commands a level of respect from our guests.

Peggy Clay, General Manager
Jo's American Bistro

The words of Johann Wolfgang van Goethe *"Character is how you treat those who can do nothing for you"* sum up how I feel about my experience in volunteering with Hugs and Halos. Most people tend to look for how the result of their actions will affect them, but you should always consider yourself to be fortunate enough to help others.

Rena DiMuccio, Volunteer VP of Development
Hugs and Halos

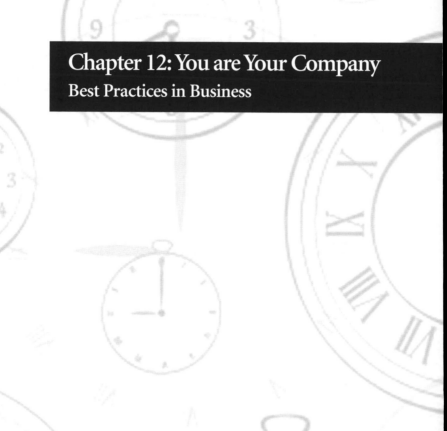

Chapter 12: You are Your Company

Best Practices in Business

Your Someday is Now.

*"When we are no longer able to change a situation -
we are challenged to change ourselves."*
- Viktor Frankl

Are you personally and professionally fulfilled with the activities in your life? Are there goals you aspire to achieve?

Start today. Do something, every day, to propel yourself forward in business and in life. In addition to your daily tasks; focus on building sustainable, successful, and sincere relationships with your internal and external "customers." Developing a network of positive, interested and supportive people in your life will assist you in fulfilling your goals.

Personally and professionally, do your best to develop a reputation for being a great asset to your company. Raise the bar beyond dependable to the "must have" employee. Why not? In the end, how you perform determines how effective and respected you are, in addition to how successful you will be.

Let's review a few best practices in the business realm.

The Penmanship Book - Write it Down

In most fine dining restaurants, the server takes your order without writing it down. Have you ever received your meal, only to discover your order was not correct? Was your meal placed in front of another person in your party? The restaurant term for this is "auctioning off" the plates.

When you go to a doctor, she or he records your history and concerns in your file. If yours does not, you may want to find a different doctor.

When you work on a project or program that requires details, and most do, outline the scope of the project. Take notes in meetings and list the action steps that you are responsible for.

When you are in charge of a project, assign clear responsibilities, with deadlines, to the others involved.

You will have busy days when you travel from appointment to appointment and meeting to meeting - the projects, messages, and proposed outcomes can become a bit confusing or overwhelming. Whew – write it down!

It is very important to listen to what people say in addition to recording the information, storing it and acting upon it. Susan Hayhurst, my friend and former client, used to joke that I carried my "penmanship book" with me to appointments. She would ask, *"What is in that book?"* She was also very pleased with our projects. When I asked her for a professional testimonial in regard to our performance, she quickly replied, *"You cannot put a price on convenience – you get it done and you get it done right!"* The "penmanship book" was instrumental in accomplishing successful programs for Susan and ultimately for Pepsi, a client of over two decades.

Make it a habit to summarize the items discussed, write them down or type them into your computer or tablet, and share the notes and action items with your colleagues and clients.

Your *follow up* will set you apart.

"Tony Soprano Management"

Knowledge is power. We have all worked with people who withhold information. In some cases, they may claim they do not have the time to stop and share notes with you from an internal meeting or external conversation with a client. They may be threatened by you or another employee and deliberately keep you uninformed.

Avoid "Tony Soprano Management," an expression I coined to express sharing a little bit of information (versus sharing the entire picture) with several different people out of fear of losing your "power" or your job.

Share the knowledge you have with your colleagues and co-workers. As David Murray, former Senior Vice President of BankNewport, professes, *"The only knowledge you keep is the knowledge you give away."* Your team, your office, and your life will be more productive when you share what you know. Moreover, you may find that others start sharing a lot more with you.

"Got a Minute?" Dealing with Interruptions

There will always be days when you desire the solitude to focus on your own work. While some people have a work environment where this is possible, in most cases, interaction with other people is inevitable.

Personally and professionally, you will always be faced with interruptions from the "got a minute's?" to the "Chatty Charlie's" and "Chatty Cathy's." On occasion, you may welcome the interruptions as a break, at other times they will be a major distraction.

When you set a deadline for a project and have organized your time to initiate your large task, here are a few suggestions to alleviate unwelcome interruptions and "keep your head in the game."

1. Arrive at the Office One Hour Early

Yikes, I know, this is a tough one! Be the first one at work. Ease into your day or jump into it, depending on your state of mind. Clear your entire desk (or a section of it) of all items except for the most important project or projects you must complete. Do not turn your email on until work "officially starts" to avoid being swept into an email vortex.

2. Start at Home with Your "To Accomplish" List

If getting to work early is impossible or if your office environment distracts you from the minute you enter, wake up an hour early, organize your day and start your projects at home.

3. Beware of Relentless Attention to Email

Turn off the "email notification" setting on your computer. In lieu of checking your emails as they "pop up," experiment with checking your email once an hour, every three hours, or twice a day. Checking and responding to emails all day is the same as answering the phone all day. Is your job description that of a receptionist or a corporate executive?

When you do open an email, take a quick glimpse and decide if it needs to be addressed immediately. Can it be "saved as new" and answered during your designated email response time? Can it be deleted, saved, forwarded or delegated?

4. Do Not Disturb

Whether you work in a private office, cubicle, or your home, set aside a period of time each day or a few days each week (whatever works best for you) when you are not to be disturbed. This can be as simple as posting a small sticky note on your door, "I just need 15 minutes." No one knows when you put the "15 minutes" sign on your door and you may end up with additional "Do Not Disturb" time!

When focused on preparing budgets, presentations, and strategies, you can also create a small sign for your door, cubicle or desk stating: "Hour of Power."

Offer the same courtesy to your co-workers – laminate and share the signs. Voila! Observe and benefit as your productivity – and that of your team – soars.

5. The Importance of Scheduling Meetings

It is productive and informative to schedule regular meetings with the people you interact with, especially your boss, your team, and your colleagues. Your meeting may be a short daily meeting, a longer weekly meeting, or a bi-monthly planning and operations meeting. Between meetings, consolidate any questions, ideas, or concerns that do not have to be addressed immediately. By "bundling" your questions to address at your meetings versus a series of "got a minute's" (in person or via email), your productivity will increase.

If you have an established meeting time with your boss or colleagues, create a list of items you would like to review. Store this list in an electronic or paper file with his or her name on it. You can also place the list in your electronic calendar under the date and time you are scheduled to meet.

More About Meetings

In the hospitality industry, many hotels commence the day with a 10 minute "standup," also referred to as "morning meeting." Gathering your team first thing in the morning for a "pow-wow" offers everyone the chance to discuss what they are working on. This brief meeting also offers the opportunity to discuss items that may require assistance from a colleague that day or later in the week. In addition to being updated in regard to what the team is working on, it is an opportunity to ask or answer questions in an effort to avoid interruptions all day long.

Ah, interruptions. Ask your team to keep a running list of questions or ideas that they can bring to the appropriate meeting versus walking into your office all day peppering you with questions. This will allow for increased productivity versus a day full of interruptions.

Meeting Management

If you do not manage meetings, meetings will manage you, which will lead to wasted time. You will get frustrated with endless meetings that do not have end results or action steps.

Prior to an internal or external meeting, prepare an agenda. Once you create an agenda, share it with the people invited to the meeting. This offers them the opportunity to prepare for the meeting and add any supplementary items. If your colleagues add to the agenda, update it and bring a copy to the meeting.

Daily, weekly, or monthly meetings provide the opportunity to relay your message, needs, and ideas to your colleagues, Board or committee members.

When you have ideas prior to the meeting, store these ideas or questions in the notes section of your electronic calendar under the meeting date. You can also create an agenda or "meeting outcome" document and add your thoughts, questions, and ideas prior to the meeting.

When you prepare your thoughts, do your best to present them as clear and concise as possible. Many people attending the meeting may not "live in your world" and they certainly do not live in your head! They may require more information on your ideas or request clarity and information.

Practice Productivity

Practice productivity every step of the way. Create "best practices" outlines or "SOP's" (Standard Operating Procedures) for your department or company and store them in one place. We all interpret and process information differently. These systems offer a step toward ensuring everyone is on the same page.

Productive and energetic meetings become meetings the team respects and looks forward to. Be known for your ability to plan and run a meeting where attendees leave energized, focused, and ready to execute their action plans. Designate a note taker at every meeting. This person should record what was discussed and outline the action plans for the team, including the people responsible for the outcomes and the dates that the tasks should be completed.

The most productive meetings become "same page" meetings - where everyone leaves on the same page with clarity and direction, in addition to an understanding of what needs to be accomplished, be it that day, week, month, or year.

Your challenges, goals and projects deserve efficient and effective use of time in order to be well thought out, reviewed, shared, and acted upon.

Quick Tips for Meeting Management.

• Avoid booking meetings back to back.

• Start on time: The moment people assume the meetings start late, they will show up later and later.

• Share an agenda.

• Set a time limit.

• Value the opinions of others - you cannot know everything.

Meeting Management Success Snapshots

1. Schedule the Meeting

Send an invitation to all of the people included in the meeting. Use Outlook or another online calendar and include the meeting time, location, and discussion points. Ask attendees to include additional items they would like to discuss.

2. Arrive Early

Be on time. In fact, arrive to the meeting 10 to 15 minutes early. If your meeting is with a client, or a prospective client, there is a great deal you can learn and observe by sitting in the lobby, waiting for the meeting. If it is an internal meeting, you will have time to talk with the other "early" attendees, catch up on correspondence, or clear your head to get focused for the meeting. It is disrespectful to arrive late to any meeting.

3. Take Charge

If you are in charge of the meeting, make sure you have an agenda prepared. Your agenda can be simple, comprised of the names of the attendees, a blank area for answers to questions, and list of items you would like to cover. When possible, distribute the agenda in advance to ensure that meeting attendees come prepared to participate.

4. Park It

When people gather for a meeting, there is often a great deal of excitement and creativity. Put unrelated topics and ideas in the "Parking Lot." Many of the best ideas for another project, product, event, or procedure come from meetings where a different topic is discussed. Use the white board, flip chart and a note taker to put those ideas on a list for a future meeting or discussion. Stay focused on the topic everyone has gathered to discuss.

5. Watch the Clock

If a meeting has been scheduled for an hour, be conscious of time and work within that time block. Before you start a meeting, especially with a new client; confirm that they have planned for ten, twenty or thirty minutes, whatever you had agreed upon when arranging the meeting.

6. Respect Opinions

When you run a meeting, make sure attendees have time to offer their input or opinion. A gregarious, opinionated person at the table may intimidate a quiet, insightful person. Do your best to ensure everyone at the table has a voice. The more ideas shared by the people in attendance, the better the outcome.

7. Follow-up

On your meeting notes, list the action plan with the person responsible and date that action must be completed. These dates can also be added to tasks on your computer. Follow up on the actions delegated.

You Are Your Company!

You represent your company to people outside the corporation. In some cases, you may be the only person that the people meet from your organization – what do you want their impression to be about you and the company you own or work with?

Reminder – you are "on stage," every minute of the day. Each new day offers you the opportunity to grow; personally and professionally. In the end, you work for you. Your grace, leadership, accomplishments and success are "yours" to carry with you as you develop in your career. Your success depends solely on what you want to put into it.

Go out there and be the BEST you!

What Are You Waiting For?

- Keep a list of projects/priorities and update it constantly.
- Plan quiet Saturday mornings in the office to think, read, write; things that are difficult to do during busy weekdays.
- Some jobs or careers do not lend themselves easily to a work life balance that would appear desirable. Make certain that if you're in one of those careers your family, spouse/partner have the same goals as you and are supportive.
- Regularly talk to, have lunch, or dinner with individuals who don't work at your company. Get as wide and diverse view of the world as you can.

Robert A. DiMuccio, President
Amica Mutual Insurance Company

Schedule regular one-on-one meetings with your staff. This will allow them a designated time to discuss any items with you and minimize the "pop-in" unscheduled meetings.

Ellen Ford, President & CEO
People's Credit Union

I arrive to work 1/2 hour before everyone else in the office. This ensures that I have quiet time to read my emails and voice mails, and review my To Do List without interruption.

Lisa Lancellotta, MBA, Coordinator, MBA Programs
University of Rhode Island
College of Business Administration

I review a list of my team members and schedule one-on-one meetings to discuss their career goals and aspirations. Although this task is not urgent, it is very important and a priority. I meet with all direct reports on a quarterly basis.

Jeffrey P. Gagnon,CPCU, Assistant Vice President Training and Development
Amica Mutual Insurance Company

Your Someday is Now.

Passed down from my Dad when I entered the work force –

"If you can be 5 minutes late for a meeting, you can be 5 minutes early." I live by this mantra. I always make sure my time is planned to ensure that I am at any meeting on time. To be late is to be selfish and not respectful of the other participant's time. This is reflected in both my professional and personal lives. Make sure you build enough time in to be at the appointed place at the appointed hour.

> John Holloran, Director, Sponsorship Marketing
> Global Headquarters
> Raytheon Company

Make lists. With all of the work you are bound to have on your plate, the easiest way to keep it all organized is a good "old fashioned" list. Keep them in order by color-coding your tasks so you know what needs to be done today (red), what needs to be done this week (black) and what can wait a few days (blue). Plus, when you're done with a task it'll feel great to cross it off the list!

> Jen Cingari, Publicist
> ESPN Films and Original Programming

"Investing time" is a great answer to saving it. Time is precious so the trick here is to invest wisely and make sure that the gains are residual. Attending "the right" training, or spending a single day teaching someone who I can delegate a project to afterwards could save me valuable time each month, every month, for years!

Also, when we are under the gun we look for short cuts and I've learned that taking the wrong ones are almost always the culprit for wasting my time. I've spent hours typing what I thought would be a quick email when I should have just picked up the phone... or, I've spent "forever" trying to fix a technology issue that support could have fixed in five minutes if I'd have only called. When deadlines are met I try to go back and evaluate what worked and what didn't and have learned how to become more proactive during "crunch time."

> Perry Kessler, Area Sales Leader
> Marriott International

I have used the following practices with multiple companies from H.J. Heinz to Welchs to Stonyfield; across sales management, sales planning and business development and they have worked well for me.

It's all about managing e-mails. I manage my in-box in Lotus notes (previously in Outlook). I have created folders that are alphabetical in Lotus notes. I use these much more than I do my document folders unless it contains a file (excel typically) that I need to update. I take action on e-mails with steps outlined below:

- Junk - delete if I am not going to need to refer to it again
- Read but might need at a later date for reference - save to appropriate folder but get it out of your in-box
- Action - any e-mail that require some action or work stays in my in-box. I use this method along with the Franklin planner that I have used now for 22 years (although not entirely the way it is intended)

In some previous positions in planning I would get as many as 100 e-mails a day. I have always been able to manage my in-box down to about 20 by the end of the week. If I have many more than that it simply means I am not keeping up with requests or projects. I also know people who have been successful with 300 or 1000 e-mails in their in-box but that is not me.

Brian Carboneau, Area Director
Stonyfield Farm

Permission to Pause –

Before a meeting, shut your door, close your eyes and take a few moments to breathe. You will be refreshed and ready for the meeting. You can also send positive energy to the attendees with wishes for the best outcome for the meeting.

Abby Murphy, Director of Development
LightBridge Hospice Community Foundation

Your Someday is Now.

Do NOT allow yourself to be comfortable. When you allow yourself to become comfortable, you are not growing. Push yourself to step out of your comfort zone every day. Make that extra cold call, run a little faster, take a chance, etc.... Over time, these little steps become leaps and bounds beyond what you ever thought possible.

Robert A. DiMuccio Jr., Sales Representative
Smith Optics

Drama has a place in all our lives but it should be invited in by you. Drama belongs in a theater, on a movie screen, on a TV. Drama should not be invited into the workplace. Who has the time to navigate through nonsense and negativity with all we are expected to accomplish in this day?

Drama breeds more drama. Nip it quick, do not let it spin and spiral out of control or it will take on a life of its own and become an unwelcome character in your workplace. The best way to downplay the drama is to "manage in the moment." Acknowledge it immediately or it will fester. Hold others accountable - put them on the spot and open up a dialogue to air out their issues. Manage the scene or it will manage you.

Be mindful that if you encourage this, you need to inspire it. You need the buy in and the only way to get it is to communicate, be authentic, check in regularly, ask for feedback and really listen to it. Assumptions are the root of drama, staying ahead of this is the key- just take a moment to educate and you will find the impact often ripples out.

Michele Maker Palmieri, General Manager
Newport Yachting Center

Chapter 13: Procrastinate Later!
Thriving on Procrastination and Dodging Delegation

Your Someday is Now.

"Nothing begins until you start."
                                -Sam Alofsin

*"If you want to make an easy job seem mighty hard,
  just keep putting off doing it."*
                                - Olin Miller

"I'll get to it later," "I am not in the mood," "I work best under pressure," "I am the only one who can do that project" - does this sound familiar? The reality is, most people procrastinate and have difficulty with delegation. Procrastination and delegation are high priority concerns.

If you truly want to tackle and master both issues, use delegation to assist with procrastination. For instance, you may be procrastinating work on a project or report that can be delegated to someone else who can do it faster, and perhaps better, than you. You may be holding on to the task due to ego or you may be too timid to ask for assistance.

Procrastinate Later!

Have you ever experienced a deadline-inspired rush of adrenalin? When on deadline, you certainly get things done – projects, final exams, and proposals. If you have to eventually get it done, why not start it now? This also applies to positive achievements you would like to add to your life – education, learning a new sport or instrument, and enjoying more time with friends and family.

I have met many people who joke about how they put the "pro" into procrastination. Now, I can understand this for projects you may not be excited about, but if you are going to do something - plan a vacation, further your education, coordinate an event or social engagement, or start an exciting and motivating project - sit down and get started.

If your project or task is not engaging or exciting, start slowly, scheduling 15 or 20 minute increments. Fold laundry while watching the news, clean a room while listening to music, a lecture or a book on your smartphone or tablet, learn a language while you walk or workout – spend time with a friend while you walk or work out. Think of a chore or project that you are avoiding. What can you "couple it" with to make it enjoyable and start today?

We all procrastinate. And procrastination is not always "bad." Get over the guilt and ask yourself why you are procrastinating. What is the cause? How will you benefit if you just start, even for 15 minutes?

The "Why"

There is an expression: *When the why is evident, the how becomes easy.* Ask yourself why the task or project is on your "to do" list. How important is it? What will beginning and completing this task do for you?

Do you want to earn an MBA, organize a fundraiser, write an article for a trade magazine, produce an event at work, or start your own company? Whatever it is, if it's on your "to accomplish" list, pick up a pen and simply outline a few action steps and a timeline. If there is a mandatory date by which the project must be completed, create your time line from this end date. If you need assistance with action steps, identify resources that can assist you (a friend, mentor, accountability coach, advice via the Internet) and plan time for these interactions as well.

Your best moments will be time spent with family, friends and faith. You never get this time back. Carve out personal time each and every day. "Someday" is now and indeed, your family, friends and faith are your most important "why's."

No Pain, No Gain

Once you start completing the tasks that will bring you to your next step in finishing a project, you may still need encouragement along the way. Most people have short attention spans and the temptation of ubiquitous technology does not help. We are tempted to check our email, surf the web, text a friend - anything but the task at hand.

Here are a few suggestions to make completion of the project and "eating those frogs," a bit more palatable:

1. Take Time to Reward Yourself

Once you begin a task or project, consider simple ways you can reward yourself during the process. You may be studying for class or preparing a presentation at work. Take a break by walking with a friend, working in your garden, attending a sporting event, stopping for a coffee, or working out at the gym.

As you gain "traction" on a project, assignment, or accomplishment – stop and congratulate yourself with a reward or positive action that means something to you.

2. The Power of Positive Thinking

Approaching life with a "yes, I can" mindset will positively impact your projects and tasks. Put your shoulders back, stand tall, and start the assignment with an optimistic frame of mind.

Every project – personal and professional – will have its challenges. Identify these challenges, acknowledge and confront them. Determine who or what can help you work through these stumbling blocks.

Practice the power of positive thinking. Try not to doubt yourself. Your mind is very powerful. Think "can," as in *"Yes, I most certainly can get this done."*

3. "Later, Gator" May Mean Never

We hear it again and again: *"I will get to it later,"* *"I will do it later,"* especially when you have a list of things you would rather be doing.

In many cases, "later" may mean you are not going to complete a project. What is holding you back? Is the project too overwhelming? If you know you can do it, yet the first step is difficult, dive in - particularly if others are waiting for your contribution to the project. Identify sources holding you back and push the task to the front burner. Ask yourself:

- Do I want to do this?
- If so, why can't I start? Is it Fear?
- Is the task too big? Is the time right?
- Do I want to avoid this? If so, can I?

Once you identify the source or sources of procrastination, create "to do" or goal sheets and add your projects and tasks to them.

4. The "Deadline Inspired" Rush of Adrenalin

Many people work better under pressure. They see the "finish line" and sprint towards it. This is the "deadline inspired, I have to do this now" counter to procrastination. While this will work in many cases, it will wear on you in the long run.

Catch Your Breath

> *"One day, in retrospect, the years of struggle will strike you as the most beautiful."* - *Sigmund Freud (1856-1939)*

There are times when you feel completely overwhelmed – whether it is at work, at home, or with your life in general. This can occur when there is an illness or death in your immediate world, during the holidays or vacation time, arrival of a new baby or puppy and sometimes just out of the blue. Give yourself permission to "shut off."

Your Someday is Now.

As a child, I spent summers in Portsmouth, Rhode Island. I loved being by the water, embracing the solitude and the long days. I recall how our neighbors walked over with their coffee, iced tea, or cocktails and sat on the porch with us, or we would walk to their porch and discuss the day, current news, family, and stories from the past. As children, we played outside all day, unless it rained and in that case we would play inside and watch a little television. We spent the day swimming, collecting shells, hiking, water-skiing, and playing board games and Barbie™ dolls. We learned to interact and get along, developing interpersonal skills.

Flash forward a few decades and we are on overload – computers, email, tablets, social media, text messages, IM, etc., both personally and professionally. We don't "shut off." We are always accessible.

While it is important in many professions and lives to be accessible 24/7, most of us should be able to find time to "shut off" – practice yoga, take a bike ride, ski, attend a child's sports practice and game, search the beach for shells, stroll through a bookstore, and simply enjoy the gift of time.

Give yourself permission to catch your breath.

Delegate with Encouragement

Perhaps you have heard the expression: *It is better to get ten people to work, than to do the work of ten!*

Delegating creates and develops leadership skills in others. We cannot know 100% of everything. Attention Mount Olympus: be aware of your limitations and learn to delegate. The workplace is no place for hubris. When you are able to share the work load, you can focus on tasks you do best – the tasks that will further your own growth and the growth of the company.

Internal partnerships with your colleagues are as important as external relationships with your clients. Do not solely delegate mundane tasks – share the exciting projects as well. As you include, you will also be included.

When you delegate, make sure to do the following:

- Pick people who can accept responsibility.
- Delegate in terms of the other person's skills and interests.
- Teach the "why" (the purpose) not just the "what."
- Appreciate the personal touch on a delegation. This will serve to *encourage* versus *discourage* the person working on the project.

Whenever possible, do only what you can do. What are your core skill sets? Where should your time be invested for the best outcome for your department or company? If you are unclear of the answer, you may want to enlist the guidance of your human resources department or business supervisor to determine this.

You will often have assignments beyond your job description. As you become aware of these tasks, determine the ones that can be delegated. If you are a department of one, request assistance from other departments or look into recruiting an intern from a local university who is interested in your field.

How to Delegate?

Let's face the facts - no one can complete a project as well as you can. However, you will never advance to the next step in your career if you do not relinquish a few of your responsibilities and commence new ones.

When you do delegate, choose people who you feel can accept the responsibility. When possible, delegate in terms of the person's skills and interests. Perhaps spreadsheets or presentations are not your favorite action item and they take you longer than they would another member of your team. Identify simple items like this, ask for assistance, and gain more efficiency and time to focus on *your* strengths, bringing additional value to the workplace.

If you are concerned about completely handing over your project – your "baby"– to another member of your team, assign a low risk project first and be patient. There will be a learning curve. Teach your colleague the "why," the purpose and the desired outcome, in addition to the "what," the action steps, and time lines of accomplishment. Be approachable and patient. This will assist in keeping lines of communication open.

Last but not least, *appreciate* the personal touch that a colleague, team member, or intern will add to a project. Be open-minded and encouraging. You may have experienced a time in your life where you added your own personal signature to a delegated task. Was it well received or discouraged by your manager? Encourage the people around you – *their* success is *your* success.

Managing Delegation

When you manage delegation, try not to hover. Keep a list of items you've assigned in addition to their priority and a due date. Take time to review the project and offer the necessary training. Request a daily, weekly, bi-monthly or monthly progress report, in writing. If a task is not up to "par" and can be detrimental to the project, review the steps towards improvement with additional encouragement.

How to Delegate?

- Pick people who can accept responsibility.
- Delegate in terms of the other persons skills and interests.
- Reduce risks by assigning low risk projects first.
- Recognize the reality of the learning curve.
- Teach the "why" (the purpose) not just the "what" (the desired outcome).
- Appreciate the personal signature on a delegation.
- Keep all lines of communication open.

Managing Delegation

- Keep a list of items assigned.
- Assign priorities and a due date.
- Provide the necessary training.
- Bring this list to meetings.
- Request a regular progress report.

Delegation Worksheet

"It is only as we develop others that we permanently succeed."

-Harvey S. Firestone

1) Pick a task – how can you get this delegated?

2) Who is the best person to delegate this to?

3) Establish the date of completion.

4) Suggest action steps for the "to accomplish" list.

5) Review a weekly progress report and offer feedback.

6) Express your appreciation.

Procrastination Worksheet

1) Your project or goal – why is it important?

2) Who or what is causing you to procrastinate on this project or goal?

3) What will completing this assignment, task, project or goal
   do for you personally or professionally?

4) What is the desired or necessary date of completion?

5) How will you break the project into small steps of
   accomplishment, tracking back from the due date?

6) Who can help you?

Your Someday is Now.

What Are You Waiting For?

My best practice for time management is to start early and to get as much as possible done before the day of the event. There are enough "exciting moments" that crop up during an event and your focus is to resolve that "moment" and not to worry about a dozen other things on your "to do" list. This is true for a variety of situations whether it is a holiday at home or a major conference which 1000 people are attending.

The day before should be your "dress rehearsal," but many things can be done months in advance. Details are important so finish the details so that they are correct well ahead of time. By doing this you eliminate a lot of stress on yourself and others around you. You can focus on the moment and the experience and not on how much you have to do.

Also you and the experience do not have to be perfect. Relax and realize when things are done well enough so that the experience is excellent, but not necessarily perfect.

> Kati Machtley, Director, The Women's Summit
> Bryant University

When it comes to your staff, whether large or small, trust them and give them latitude. Trust them to do it and let them do it their way. Now it is off your plate. Too many people stay involved. If you move from marketing VP to COO, let the new marketer do the job in his or her way. Let him or her be the person they are. You cannot micro-manage when you are a step higher.

> Larry Cancro, Senior VP of Fenway Affairs
> Boston Red Sox

If you can complete something on your "to do" list in 2 minutes or less.... DO IT NOW! You will get a great sense of accomplishment by checking even small things off your list and reduce the constant movement of papers, piles, post its and thoughts from one place to another for future follow up.

> Randy Schreiber, President
> GutterBrush Guys Ltd.

As a manager, make sure to notice and acknowledge publicly the small things that those who work for you do well. Quick and short positive feedback to note when someone takes initiative and/or does something well goes a long way in making the individual feel like what they are doing is being noticed and gives them the confidence to do it again, allowing them to release their potential. So often managers only acknowledge the big stuff, and although good, this often has less impact than noticing the small, positive things people do along the way that make the big end project a success!

Kathleen Kits van Heyningen, Senior Director- Creative & Customer Experience
KVH

Don't put anything off, as it will multiply with every passing day!

Paul Trudeau, Director of Retail, South/Central US
Voss Water

Admit when you need help. I delegate a job or hire someone temporarily to help me get the jump on a large task that has been relegated to the procrastination closet. It forces me to make the time commitment, organize the task, and makes me feel more accomplished when I push it out the door.

Kimi Puntillo, Principal
KP Communications

Like many small business owners with a keen eye on the bottom line, in order to save money at times, I tended to be a bit of a "do it yourselfer," "I can do this," and "I can figure this out," often in areas where I was hardly qualified.

As time is money, I hate to think how much money I have wasted by spending valuable time on tasks that could have been completed much more efficiently and in the long run far more economically had I hired the appropriate professional needed right from the beginning. My short answer to time management is "When in doubt...hire out."

Suzi Conklin Nance, President
Capitol Realty Company

Your Someday is Now.

When facing a pile of projects with a due date, always complete the project on the top of the pile first. If you place something you really don't want to complete on the bottom, it continues to rise to the top. Completing those tasks first will set you free.

Susan Hayhurst Boscia, President
SalesUp & Associates

Overwhelmed at home? Just Start!

- Use two laundry baskets - dark one for dark laundry and a white one for everything else. Teach your children at a young age to separate their clothes into dark and white baskets

- Load the washing machine the night before so all you have to do in the morning is put in detergent and start.

- Everyone is rushing around in the morning to leave the house so do as much as you can the night before – Set the coffee maker, lay out clothes, etc.

- Keep a shopping bag in your closet for clothes that you want to give to the Goodwill or consignment store

- Always keep a loaf of bread in the freezer (and a bottle of wine in the refrigerator!)

- When making doctors appointments, always ask for the first appt of the day or the first one after lunch. That way the doctors won't be running behind, hopefully.

Mary Ellen Schuttenhelm, Domestic Goddess
CEO of the Schuttenhelm Organization

When you have many tasks on hand, make a list and prioritize and tackle them one at a time. Crossing a completed task off your list gives you a sense of accomplishment and motivation to move forward. It also helps keep your mind clear to focus on what's in front of you. Replenish and re-organize your list every day to keep the process current and moving forward. If you have someone available to help, use them. It empowers them, builds their confidence, gives you a "go to" and helps you with your ultimate goal of "moving the ball forward."

John L. Capone, Senior Counsel and Patent Attorney
Duffy & Sweeney, Ltd.

Do it right, do it once, do it now!

> Tom Foley, SVP, Mortgage Origination
> The Mortgage Corner of New England

What I do that helps me immensely is that I try to think about tasks only once before deciding when to do them. For example, if I know I need to make or change a doctor's appointment, I either do it immediately- taking that 5 minutes only once. If their office isn't open or I'm otherwise engaged, I will write it down- ideally on my calendar for a specific date on which I will do it.

If it's something that can't or shouldn't be done right away and doesn't have a date associated with it, it goes on the general "to-do" list but I keep my "to-do" list to specific actionable tasks (not eat healthier, save money, volunteer more) and work my way down it as efficiently as I can opting to do some of the things as soon as I read them, rather than read them multiple times and transfer them from list to list.

> Alyson Singer, Producer
> Boston, MA

As a long time Boy Scout leader, I think back to our troop's very first campout. Our youngest patrol announced they were going to make toast on the campfire for breakfast. A horrified parent took me aside saying "You can't make toast on a campfire! You have to tell them."

My response was "One of two things will happen. Either they will put a piece of bread on a stick, scorch it on the fire and it will be completely inedible. Or, they will find a way to weave some sticks together to hold the bread and actually toast it on the coals. Either way they will have learned something."

> Scott Fraser, Principal
> Fraser Communications

Your Someday is Now.

Chapter 14:
Leadership Grace and Growth
The Power of Positivity

*"The secret of life, though, is to fall seven times and
to get up eight times."*

-*Paulo Coelho*

A positive mindset will always save you time. My Aunt Terry Merrill has always counseled us not to "waste a good worry." Why waste a minute worrying about the things you cannot change, the people who do not appreciate you, or situations that need adjustment? Start today by doing *your* best to change *your* outlook on the world. This is the ultimate time-saver.

Turning "Oops" Into Opportunity

Failure is important along your path to achievement. You learn valuable lessons from failure. Think about the people you know who embrace their mistakes and learn from them. Can you think of one person who has had success his or her entire life without having worked for it? Success can emerge from great failure and conquer dire circumstances. Continue to remind yourself that failure is not in the falling down, it is in the staying down. Turn "oops" into opportunity.

We all know people who live in the past. Perhaps they stress the positive: *"Those were the days," "Life was simpler then,"* or *"We had so much fun."*

They may reflect negatively: *"I was denied a childhood," "My sister teased me incessantly," "My second grade teacher put soap in my mouth,"* or *"My mother liked my siblings better than she liked me."* Whatever your past may have been, it is time to face forward and create your future.

Learn from the past and look forward in life! Think about it: when you drive your car, you look out the front windshield, glancing at the rear-view mirror to check the road behind you. However, if you are going to turn around for an extended view, it would be prudent to stop the car. It is fine to look in the rear-view mirror as long as you are well aware that your destination and your future lies *ahead* of you. While you cannot change the past, you *can* focus on taking steps to create a fulfilling future.

At times, you will make errors. You can refer to these times as "What was I thinking?" moments. Stop and reflect – would you truly do anything different under the exact same circumstances? And, if you would, reconcile this within yourself and move forward.

We tend to berate ourselves. We lose weeks, months, and years of sleep, pining about mistakes made in the past. It is a waste of time to stay focused on your mistakes. *Bless and release* – establish closure and move on.

"Collect" People

No one can be an expert on everything, try as they may. There are people who may think they are an authority on all subjects; "legends in their own minds."

We all have our special gifts, in addition to subjects that we have concentrated on and specialized in. What do you want to be an expert in? Have you demonstrated the aptitude, interest, or talent? Are there people who can help you?

Collect people. Create your own personal "board of advisors." Ideally, this "board" will be comprised of people who can help you in a select field or personal area of focus. These people may become your mentors for a brief period, or for your entire life. They may be people who you know peripherally or personally. They might even be people that you follow on the Internet and via social media – famous, successful, and insightful people who share interests similar to yours.

What kind of mentors do you need? That will depend on what you deem necessary in your life at the given moment. You may want to have several, including a spiritual mentor who assists you with reflecting on personal and professional decisions. You may want to have several business mentors who assist you with insight and introductions throughout your career.

Your Someday is Now.

You will welcome different mentors throughout the chapters of your life. Focus on spiritual, educational, business and financial mentors to start. You can include an "attitude" mentor if you find yourself in need of a positive influence.

Who do you have in your life who is able to assist you in your personal and professional growth?

Be a Positive Role Model

There is no better way to learn than to teach. Who can *you* instruct and mentor? Whose life can *you* make a positive impact on? Our greatest influence is through the lessons taught by our actions. My mother always counseled us that we may be the only Bible that people read. Talk about pressure!

Eeyore, Where's Your Tail?

We have all known people, personally or professionally, who enter the office or social setting with their shoulders slumped and head down, analogous to Eeyore, the donkey featured in A.A. Milne's classic, *Winnie the Pooh.*

If you ever feel like Eeyore, how can you adjust your mind set? Do you want the reputation of having a negative personality? Do you want to be a person who empties other people's "buckets" of optimism or internal spirit? Once you have a reputation for this kind of personality, it becomes your personal brand.

We all have bad days. If you are having a bad day, *every* day, it is time to take a good look at your life, your job, and your personal situation. If your situation is truly dire, you may want to seek professional assistance, and it is available.

However, if you *have it all* – starting with your health – be grateful. Take nothing for granted.

Live in Your Song

Years ago, I presented at a corporation in New Hampshire and asked the attendees for their input on how they "snap out" of a bad mood. One young lady, mid-twenties, raised her hand and mentioned that her challenge had been listening to the radio during her drive to work. When she was a few minutes away from her office, she would hear a sad love song reminding her of a former beau. This could alter her mood for the morning or entire day.

To "snap out of it," she purchased the cassette *"My Sharona"* (I am dating myself!) and listened to this song, every day, when she was three minutes away from her office. After parking her car, she put her shoulders back and strutted into work humming *"My Sharona."* It put her in a positive mood for the entire day. How could it not?

What song inspires you and instantly gets you in a great mood?
Live in *your* song.

Upbeat and Inspiring Songs

What a Wonderful World (Louis Armstrong)
Dancing in the Moonlight (King Harvest)
Love Shack (B52's)
Saturday in the Park (Chicago)
Ho Hey (The Lumineers)
Your Smiling Face (James Taylor)
Fly Me to the Moon (Frank Sinatra)
Don't Worry, Be Happy (Bobby McFerrin)
Who Loves You (Frankie Valli and the Four Seasons)
Moondance (Van Morrison)
Viva La Vida (Cold Play)
Babylon (David Gray)
Takin' It to the Streets (Doobie Brothers)
Here Comes the Sun (The Beatles)
I'm So Excited (Pointer Sisters)
C'mon Get Happy (The Partridge Family)
Sweet Caroline (Neil Diamond)

Your Someday is Now.

Snap Out of It!

> *"…the greater part of our happiness or misery depends on our dispositions and not on our circumstances."*
>
> -Martha Washington, First Lady

Every now and then you have to ask yourself, *"Is it me?"* Take charge and master your moods. A bad mood is a notorious waste of time, so here are a few ideas to "snap out of it."

Your "Snap Out of It" Check list!

- Surround yourself with positive things and people, for instance: books that interest you, motivational CDs or MP3 downloads, "feel good" movies, cheerful friends, positive acquaintances.

- Embrace the elements – rain, wind, snow or sun. Take a walk or go to the gym. Relax by a fire or just go outside and enjoy a breath of fresh air.

- Laugh, whether you are alone or with a friend. Watch a comedy or read a funny book. Dance and sing in your living room – with others or alone!

- Become an active volunteer. When you serve others and work with the less fortunate, you will appreciate the gifts you have been given.

- Do something you are good at – sports, art, theater, music, gardening.

- Call or visit with someone who thinks you are remarkable. Yes, you can call your mother!

- Make a list of your talents and accomplishments and a list of the people and blessings in your life that make you happiest. Refer to this list when you have down moments.

- Choose a career that you love. It will make getting up and going to work much more palatable.

- Save the complimentary letters and thank you notes you have received, store them in a safe area, and read them on a "rainy" day.

Mirror, Mirror

My sister, Jennifer, mother of four, amazing wife, fitness guru and full-time orthodontist keeps a yellow piece of paper taped to her bathroom mirror that reads:

> *"I am not going to let ANYONE or ANYTHING ruin my day today."*

Inspired by Dr. Wayne Dyer, these words offer an encouraging start to her day.

I added this note to my mirror a few years ago and it reminds me, every day, to commence each day with a most positive mindset.

Chase Away the Blues

> *"You may not be able to control the situation, but you can always control your reaction."* - Austin McGonigle

One of my older friends asserts she would not trade any of the broken hearts she has experienced over the years. Broken hearts and broken promises teach us invaluable lessons.

That said, there are times that you feel "blue" and want to chase these feelings away. The feelings may stem from conflict at work, home, or with friends. They may just be inside you.

Here are a few ideas that may help you to truly live every heartbeat:

1) Surround yourself with positive people and environments.

2) Volunteer for non-profit groups – pass out water at walks and runs, stuff envelopes, do data entry, help with registration.

3) Join a board or committee of a non-profit organization. You will become aware of many people who are less fortunate than you. Identify and offer your strengths to the organization.

Your Someday is Now.

Serve Others

My parents have dedicated their lives to serving the less fortunate through their talents and treasure (donations). They have always encouraged us to volunteer via their words, leadership, and actions. The importance of serving others is a cornerstone for our family.

Our volunteer work commenced at a young age. In 4th and 5th grade at St. Joseph's School in Norwich, CT, we sold items ranging from 25 cents to $5 to raise money for missionaries in the Third World. We took this very seriously, going door to door in our neighborhood, selling the religious items. Our teachers informed us that our fundraising efforts assisted families who were less fortunate, by providing the basics of food and shelter.

My years as a Girl Scout were among the most positive of my childhood. In addition to learning people skills and sales skills by selling cookies door to door, I learned how to set meaningful goals through the badge program. I was introduced to sincere and natural networking, reinforced through the song *"Meet new friends, but keep the old   one is silver and the other gold."*

As a 17–year-old Literacy Volunteer, I met people twice my age who did their grocery shopping by looking at the picture of the food items on the cans - quite an awakening at a young age.

Another childhood memory was washing dishes at the local Cancer Home. My mom, a Registered Nurse, volunteered at the home, feeding the patients and assisting with a variety of medical tasks. She asked us to clear, wash and put away the cups and dishes from the trays by the patients' bed. We enjoyed meeting the patients and listening to their life stories. These visits illustrated early in life that indeed, we had nothing to complain about. We stopped complaining about the pimples on our face and were grateful that we had a face. Amen!

In Pursuit of Happiness

What is the quickest "prescription" for happiness?

Help other people who are less fortunate – volunteer for one or several non-profit organizations and share your gifts – whether it is the gift of time, talent or treasure. Make a small difference, and continue to make another and another. It will become part of the fabric of who you are and you will be a very happy and fulfilled person. We can all make a difference, one person or non-profit initiative at a time.

One of my favorite stories is the *Story of the Starfish*.

The story features a young boy walking on a beach littered with thousands of starfish, washed up on the shore following a storm. He relentlessly picks up the starfish as fast as he can, throwing them back into the ocean. An older man walks by and scoffs at the young boy, asking him why he bothers to throw any of the starfish back into the ocean. In fact, the older man expounds that it will not make a difference. The young man, standing his ground, tosses another starfish into the ocean and replies: *"Well sir, it certainly made a difference to that one."*

Focus on how *you* can make a difference, every day, in the lives of others. *That* is the secret to happiness.

Personal Leadership – Life is More than Playing the Part of Elsa

One of the earliest leadership lessons I learned was at the tender age of 17. From my freshman year in high school, I participated in every school play. I loved the stage and being a part of the drama team. In my senior year, our Drama Club collectively chose a classic and one of my all time favorites – *The Sound of Music* – for the spring play.

There was one hitch. The drama teacher I had worked with for the first three years had passed away and we had a new, experienced actress as the director of the drama department. She was professional – you earned your roles- no entitlement and no resting on laurels. She was a change agent!

My mindset, however, was one of entitlement. I had it all figured out. My best friend, Mardy, had a beautiful voice. She would have the role of Maria. I would have the role of "Elsa," the baroness. After all, she was blonde in the movie.

Auditions took place and the results were posted. As I reviewed the posting, I saw my name, Gail Lowney, under the title "Stage manager." Hmm, I thought, they must have a great deal of faith in me to give me the position of Stage Manager and the role of Elsa.

As I kept reading, I gasped! My other best friend, Alyson, had been chosen for the role of Elsa. How could it be? She did not tell me she had auditioned for the part. And – Alyson had brown hair! Stage Manager – what an insult!

And then…the Oprah "AHA" moment!

What I learned over the weeks of preparation was that being the Stage Manager was a tremendous opportunity to learn so many new aspects of theatre. Additionally, I was able to work with Alyson, who gave an excellent performance as Elsa and Mardy who was captivating as Maria.

I learned there is more to life than playing the part of Elsa. I learned the importance of celebrating other people's talents – their talents do not make you "less than." The evolution from "on stage" to "backstage" was enlightening and a new learning experience.

Change is growth and being the "star" of a show does not mean you always have to be on the stage – front and center. There is great value behind the scenes.

A New You - Be Your Own Hollywood!

"I think of life itself now as a wonderful play that I've written for myself, and so my purpose is to have the utmost fun playing my part."

- Shirley MacLaine

A New YOU!

List the attributes, characteristics, and strengths of a person or people you would like to emulate in order to attain your goals:

1)

2)

3)

A New YOU!

What are three time management and positive thinking actions that you can do each day to make it a GREAT day?

1)

2)

3)

A New YOU!

What are three positive Time Management habits you will work to develop?

1)

2)

3)

Your Someday is Now.

What Are You Waiting For?

Live Life Like It's Supposed To Work: Live life everyday with the mindset that whatever happens: good, bad, exciting or depressing - are all things that are meant to happen. Live everyday like it is supposed to work out, live - like you are going to meet and surpass your goals, live - like your greatest dreams will be fulfilled along with dreams that you haven't even dreamt yet. These bumps in the road during the normal day - yes - they are supposed to be there because this road leads you to where you are supposed to be going. Wake up tomorrow, walk, talk and act like life is supposed to work.....and it will.

Scott Cohen
Ogilvy – New York

Patience with Persistence

One of my favorite quotes goes like this, *"Be not afraid of changing slowly, be only afraid of standing still."* After searching I couldn't find an author for the quote, but it's become a motto of mine, almost a way of being, so much so that I have it on my fridge as a daily reminder. In a world where instant gratification for self-improvement, career growth or every day communication is demanded we often forget the authenticity, and quite frankly, the beauty in patience...with persistence. Patience with persistence is what I like to think as the happy medium between allowing life to let things happen, and shaping it on your own enough to make it happen. It's keeping focused, while being open enough to let real growth and change truly grow and transform at a pace where it becomes everlasting.

Cassandra Lukeris Earle, Regional Marketing Manager
Hyatt Regency Newport Hotel & Spa

Innovation usually comes from outside our scope of vision, so we must be intent on opening our eyes and minds wider if we are to experience success. If we aren't making mistakes we aren't making progress. Every day can't be a game day or we will never get better at what we do. We have to take time to practice, to hone our skills, to re-balance, or by the fourth quarter we haven't anything left to give.

Eleanor Warmack, Executive Director
Florida Recreation and Park Association, Inc.

Start Each Day Fresh! Start each day with a positive fresh perspective, do not worry that you did not get everything done the day before or that you had a disagreement with someone or something did not go your way. Wake up, wipe the slate clean and begin your day with energy, commitment and an enthusiastic attitude. Being positive is productive and contagious!

Wendy Kagan, SVP, Director of HR
BankNewport

Once you have a job, it is still important to reach out, make connections and get information, especially when you identify people willing to help you. It's similar to tennis: If you are up 40-Love, you can play a loose point or two and still be okay, but it is exactly those at those types of times that you want to be especially focused. One or two errors can creep in and all of a sudden it's deuce, and there is more pressure because you had a lead and did not capitalize when you could have. Now you have to work twice as hard as the other guy is caught up and energized. On top of losing your previous advantage because you relaxed, you also lost your self discipline and let your guard down.

It's important to treat every point like it's a match point and every networking opportunity like it's the one that could get you the job; because who knows, a couple of years down the road, it could do just that.

Like Warren Buffett once said, *"When people are greedy, be fearful and when people are fearful, be greedy,"* so I really try to embody that when it comes to fighting natural instincts and making the most of an opportunity, not matter how far down the road that opportunity has a chance of materializing.

Andrew McHugh, Customer Service Associate
Google

Speak your mind. No matter how young or old, tall or small, experienced or inexperienced you are, don't be scared to speak up. Whether it's a question that seems silly or your opinion, chances are, you're not the only one thinking it. Get your voice out there and be heard.

Samantha Pincins, Auditor - Officer within Corporate Audit
State Street Corporation

Your Someday is Now.

Chapter 15: YOUR Someday is NOW!

"Ancora Imparo" (I am Still Learning)

Your Someday is Now.

*"Our battered suitcases were piled on the sidewalk again;
we had longer ways to go. But no matter, the road is Life."*
- Jack Kerouac

Ancora Imparo is Italian for "I am still learning."

"Commencement" means beginning. Lifelong learning is crucial. You are more interesting when you talk about intelligent subjects (*i.e. news, history, current events*) and interests, rather than gossip and minutia.

Learning involves more than reading the paper or watching the news. Perhaps procuring a degree or improving on a skill is a goal for you? Take a week, month, year, or years to enhance skills that interest you and will serve to develop your expertise, marketability and happiness.

To be successful in time management and work life integration or balance is to *redefine* what is important and *realign* your priorities. You will be happiest when you are not thinking about being happy. Enjoy the world around you and focus on what you do have - the gifts of health, love, career, true friends – you will realize that you live in abundance versus scarcity.

Happiness is not a "when," it is a "now." Participate in situations where you will experience joy and avoid people who do not bring out the best in you.

Be conscious of the "myth of more." More money and more things will not bring you more happiness. Your attitude and appreciation set the foundation for happiness. And happiness is success - be successful now.

To realign your priorities and redefine "Importance," I offer a few final thoughts.

1) The Pareto Principle – The 80/20 Rule

The Pareto Principle is also referred to as the 80-20 rule. It was named after the Italian economist, Vilfredo Pareto, who observed that 80% of the wealth in Italy was controlled by 20% of the population. His research concluded that, in most cases, 80% of results come from 20% of the action towards garnering those results.

We can divide our day-to-day decisions and activities into the vital and the minutiae. Here are a few examples to illustrate the Pareto Principle in action:

- 20% of the products or services you sell account for 80% of your sales.

- 20% of your customers (and in some cases your employees!) contribute to 80% of your success in business.

- 80% of your problems come from 20% of the people you know! (And then some!)

- 80% of the clothes you wear come from 20% of your wardrobe. (Hmmm….gives a whole new meaning to "less is more.")

To utilize the Pareto Principle in a few aspects of your life, ask yourself:

"What 20% could you do with YOUR time that will account for 80% of the value of this time?

Nothing is 100%. Be thankful for the 80% of your life, career, activities and relationships that are positive versus focusing on the 20% that aggravate you. For instance, list the reasons you like your job, in addition to the things you would like to change. You can make this same list for your personal life. "Pareto Principle" the activities in your life that are important to you.

Your Someday is Now.

2) If You Will Do it Later, Why Not Do it Now?

This question applies to projects, deadlines, achievements, education, and hobbies. Identify the true source of procrastination. Is it fear, doubt, time, resources? Heads up! When the "why" is strong enough, the "how" becomes easy.

3) Why Wrestle with a Pig?

While you cannot teach attitude, you can influence it by your own actions. People are watching you. Be kind. Do your best not to "step on" people. They may have abusive people in their lives or an unfortunate circumstance that is not visual. Everyone has "stuff" in his or her life.

Try not to waste time "wrestling with a pig." Why? The pig is already dirty and you will get dirty too. Flame the right flames - don't waste your time on minutiae. Stay clean – it will serve to aggravate the pig even more!

4) Finishing School - Knowledge is Everywhere

When my *Memere* (French for "grandmother") was growing up, it was popular for women to attend "finishing school" where they would learn skills such as home economics and etiquette. She raised her eleven children to be thoughtful, kind and successful individuals, including her eldest child, my father. She excelled in the area of family.

Aim to be the best. Be known as the "Hall of Fame" in your field! Keep your personal skills sharp with a focus on lifelong education and improvement.

Every day, do something to increase your brain power. Listen to the news. Read the newspaper, magazines, blogs or web articles. Listen to podcasts. Stay educated and stay current. Observe your surroundings – billboards, bus shelters advertising, and a variety of marketing mediums.

As I mentioned earlier, my mother always told us that the most interesting people ask *you* about *you*. Be interested in other people.

5) Give More, Get More

It is important to approach each day with the attitude of "*What can I give?*" rather than "*What can I get?*"

Look beyond yourself. There is a whole other world out there and people need you, your expertise, your spirit and your gifts. Share the talents that you have been blessed with. Be a mentor, advisor, teacher and role model.

6) Be Where You Are

When I was graduating from college, I was convinced that being anywhere and everywhere except living in my home town was "the answer." My father offered this poignant wisdom:

> "*When you are in one place and long to be in another – it is not a matter of the place, it is what you are looking for inside.*"

Why not be present, in the moment…as completely as you can be?
BE where you ARE.

7) Gratitude

Start your day with an appreciative mindset. In short, enjoy every day, with who you have, the best you can.

When you feel yourself getting a bit blue, focus on an important question: *What do I have to be thankful for today?*

Your answers may include your great family, friends, positive environment (personal and professional), education, job, career, hobbies, vacation memories and new holidays planned.

Stop and say 'thank you' for the fact that you woke up today. One of my older friends, Sister Ernestine, is thankful for every day that she wakes up and knows her name!

Show appreciation – personally and professionally. It takes a minute to say *"Good morning," "Good afternoon," "Great to see you,"* and *"Thank you."*

In the end, peace at work and home will supply an incredible sense of balance.

8) *Lagniappe*

Lagniappe is defined as "a little something extra." My husband, a graduate of Tulane University in New Orleans, shared the story of a local coffee shop that sold beignets by the dozen. The locals knew which sales associate's line to get into for an unadvertised "baker's dozen" (13 beignets) for the price of a dozen. With a quick wink, the associate would toss an extra beignet into his bag.

Lagniappe can also be defined as the splash of rum that your grandmother might put in her banana bread prior to baking it, or an extra spice your aunt adds to her "famous" soup.

Lagniappe is not a replacement for exemplary work or service - it is that icing on the cake and, in most cases, it is what your friends, families and clients will remember.

What *Lagniappe* can you add to the lives of others today?

9) Bookmarks

> *"Don't search for the answers...live the questions...*
> *Live your way into the answer."* -Rainer Marie Rilke

Do you ever feel like you have "lost your place?"

Most of us have experienced this, more than once. Flip through the pages of your life and you will find it again – your place, that is! It may take time and is worth the time.

What are you waiting for in order to live your dreams? Enough clients? A cool job? More money? Prince or Princess Charming?

There is no time to wait. YOUR time is now. LIVE every heartbeat!

10) The Invisible Sign

Flashback to eighth grade: Sister Theresita Donach ("Sister T") taught us to practice being kind to people we met – whether it was at the grocery store, library or soup kitchen. She asked us to envision people wearing a sign that read: *Make me feel important.*

Show your character. Stop to say hello, instead of talking on your phone at the drycleaners or coffee shop. Take a minute to smile and to be polite. Etiquette is an important quality in your quest for an admirable professional and personal brand. Practice your emotional intelligence on a daily basis.

11) The Tallest Tree

Sister T also taught us that there are two ways to be the *"Tallest Tree in the Forest."* The first way is simple: you cut all the other trees down. Now you are certainly the tallest.

The better way is to sink your roots in deep and foster the growth of the trees around you. *Encourage* the other trees, build them up and provide the best fertilizer of positive intentions and lessons for their success.

This way, you will have a strong "forest" of support when the winds, the rain and the other elements arrive on the scene. Your goal is to be a "tall tree." Now, how will you get there?

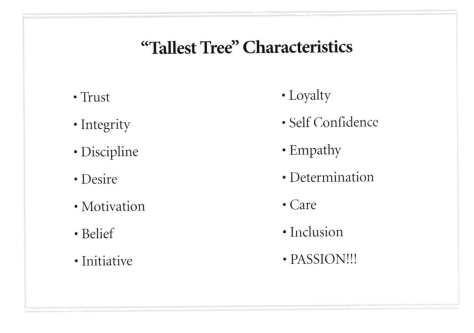

"Tallest Tree" Characteristics

- Trust
- Integrity
- Discipline
- Desire
- Motivation
- Belief
- Initiative

- Loyalty
- Self Confidence
- Empathy
- Determination
- Care
- Inclusion
- PASSION!!!

12) YOUR Someday is NOW!

What plans would you have if you knew you could not fail?

Create a life where you wish there were more hours in one day. Build your life on what you are passionate about. Be a walking "exclamation point" - enthusiastic and APPRECIATIVE of the blessings in your life! Focus on the positive things in your workplace versus the negative. When you like what you are doing, it becomes who you are.

Life is too short to worry about making a bed, ironing a shirt, or washing the floor...LIVE!

It is so important to be kind to yourself. We can often be our harshest critics. Celebrate little victories alone and as a team. Often the effort itself is the victory.

In the words of F. Scott Fitzgerald:

> *"I hope you live a life you're proud of. If you find that you're not, I hope you have the strength to start all over again."*

Yes, you can do it all....but not all at once.

YOUR "Someday" is now! What are YOU waiting for?

A Final Note

Whether enjoying my career as a sales and marketing executive for Newport Harbor Corporation, adjunct professor at the University of Rhode Island, keynote speaker and seminar leader at a conference or corporation, volunteer for several charities in the United States and the poor of Haiti, or spending time with my faith, family, friends and community; my purpose, passion and inspiration focus on one thing – making a difference.

Blessed with a healthy mind and body, today, it is my opportunity, versus obligation, to share the gifts that I have to offer and live my life with purpose and gratitude.

My wish for you is that you are able to share your gifts, your passion and your resources to make a difference in this world. This is the true secret to happiness.

The time is now. Your Someday is NOW.
What are YOU waiting for?

Wishing you the very best life has to offer!

Gail Lowney Alofsin
www.gailspeaks.com
gail@gailspeaks.com
twitter@gailspeaks/twitter@gailalofsin

Insight and Wisdom from Friends and Colleagues

Thank you to my friends, family, clients, colleagues and students who have contributed their knowledge and experience to this book via the *"What Are You Waiting For?"* section in the back of chapters one through fourteen.

The insight they have shared is most appreciated.
Their friendship, invaluable.

Mark Adams

Renata Adams

John Alofsin

Samuel Alofsin

Nancy Andrade

Jim Andrews

Amanda Barker

Nora Beger

Nicole Bertrand

PJ Boatwright

Susan Hayhurst Boscia

Andrew Botieri

Erica Brandler

Allie Brickman

Krista Bridges

Blanca Brown

Vince Burks

Larry Cancro

John Capone

Brian Carboneau

Marie Casale

Kathleen Charbonneau

Wayne Charness

Kate Chroust

Jen Cingari

Laura Clark

Peggy Clay

Scott Cohen

Terri Conners

R. Kyle Conway

Brian Cotsonas

Liz Zima Cottrell

Marie Cuccia

Michelle Davidson

Joseph DiMuccio

Rena DiMuccio

Robert A. DiMuccio

Robert A. DiMuccio Jr.

Dan Dipiro

Pam Dipiro

Sister Theresita Donach

TJ Donovan

Nancy Drinkwater

Susan Tracy-Durant

Cassie Lukeris Earle

Kathryn Farrington

Danielle Fay

Tom Foley

Ellen Ford

Margie Fox

Mike Fraioli

Scott Fraser

Tracy Freese

Frances Young Fuchs

Jeffrey Gagnon

Mark Glazier

Larry Gulko

Rob Hamilton

Robin Harmon

Amy Haughey

Brian Heil

Shannon Heil

Mark Hellendrung

John Henley

Brian Hill

John Holloran

Colleen Hopkins

David Izzo

Wendy Kagan

Daphne Kalaidjian

Amie Kershaw

Perry Kessler

Kathleen Kits van Heyningen

Wendy Kopp

Natalia Kuziw

Lisa Lancellotta

Rebecca Knapp LeBlanc

Erminia (Meme) Lindsay

"Wisdom is not a product of schooling but of the lifelong attempt to acquire it." - *Albert Einstein*

Jennifer Lowney
Jeremiah Lowney
Kristine Lowney
E. Marilyn Lowney
Mark X. Lowney
Virginia Lowney
Kathryn Whitney Lucey
Annie Sherman Luke
Michael Lynch
Donna Mac
Michelle Lowney MacDonald
Kati Machtley
Danielle Stead Mancuso
Mike Martone
Andrew McHugh
Ann Marie McLaughlin
Teresa Winiarski Merrill
Keith Miranda
Julie A. Montalbano
Angela Moore
Scott Morin
Abby Murphy
Amy Murphy-St. Laurent
Suzi Conklin Nance
NIROPE (Nick, Ron and Peter Cardi)

Brittany Noble
Ryan Nolan
Chuck O'Connor
J. Timothy O'Reilly
Paul O'Reilly
Annie Oster
Chuck Paiva
Michelle Maker Palmieri
Judi Palmer
Lenny Panaggio
Samantha Pincins
Lisa Pratt
Mardy Watts Prestley
Kimi Puntillo
Victoria Revier
Thomas Riel
Christopher J. Robertson
Diane Rocco
Joe Rocco
Brooke Rodriguez
Howard Samuels
Blakeley Schmidt
Randy Schreiber
Mary Ellen Schuttenhelm
Rich Schuttenhelm
Luke Sessa

Barbara Shea
Stewart Silvestri
Steve Sisneros
Alyson Singer
Evan Smith
Sheryl Spanos
Dawn Speros
Nancy Staples
Beth Steucek
Gary Stiffler
Don Troppoli
Paul Trudeau
Karen Van Dongen
Mary Kay Vrba
Tiffany Hodes Waddell
Brendon Walsh
Nina Walsh
Eleanor Warmack
Sharon Hoyle Weber
Janine Weisman
Robert Wolfkiel
Carolyn Woodis
Kendra Wright
Michael Young

About Authentic Measurable Performance (AMP!)

As the Founder and President of Authentic Measurable Performance (AMP!), Gail Lowney Alofsin brings her enthusiasm, inspiration, passion, ENERGY and knowledge as a speaker and educator to national and international conferences and corporations. Her Professional Development topics include: Personal and Professional Leadership, Time Management, Work/Life Balance and Integration, Personal Branding, Customer Service, Sales & Marketing, Spirit in the Workplace and The Power of Positivity!

Gail's has presented seminars and keynotes at conferences, associations and corporations including:

Advanced Results Marketing

AGSES (Association of Girl Scout Executive Staff)

American Marketing Association

American Mussel Harvesters

Amica Mutual Insurance

Aon eSolutions

Arthritis Foundation

Biogen

Blue Cross Blue Shield RI

Bonnier Corporation

Borderfest - Hildago

Brown University Medical School

Brown University Women in Medicine

Bryant University Women's Summit

Buffalo Events Network

CFEA (Colorado Festival and Events Association)

Clear Channel Radio

Clements' Market

Cox Communications

Crime Stoppers International

CSS (Center for Sales Strategy)

DCI (Drum Corps International)

DMC Network

Family Orthodontic Care

FFEA (Florida Festival & Events Association)

FRPA (Florida Recreation & Parks Association)

Gilbane Construction

GMAC (Graduate Management Admission Council)

Hall Communications

HD Smith Pharmaceuticals

Headquarters Air Education and Training Command

Hudson Valley Tourism

IEG (International Events Group)

IFEA (International Festivals and Events Association)

IFFS (International Film Festival Summit)

IMFCON (International Music Festival Conference)

International Tennis Hall of Fame

ISEN (Illinois Special Events Network)

Johnson & Wales Professional Development

Johnson & Wales Strategic Planning

KSL Television and Radio

MARC (Midwest Anesthesia Residents Conference)

Marriott - Global

Marriott - Newport

MassMutual Financial Group

Matlet Group

Memorial Hospital

MetLife Foundation National Arts Forum Series

MFEA (Michigan Festival and Events Association)

MGM Grand

MPINE (Meeting Professionals International New England)

NABA (National Association of Black Accountants)

National Association of Realtors

National Concierge Association

National Cox Television Convention

New England Dairy Council

NEHRSA (New England Health, Racquet, Sportsclub Association)

NEIRA (New England Inns & Resorts Association)

NE/SAE (New England Society of Association Executives)

Newport Chamber of Commerce

Newport CVB

Newport Hospitality

Newport Public Library

New London County Dental Society

Northeast Delta Dental

Northeastern University MBA Program

NRPA (National Recreation and Park Assoc.)

Nuance Communications

Oglebay National Training Center

Panera Bread

People's United Bank

PMPI (Potomac Chapter of Meeting Professionals International)

Potter League for Animals

Providence Warwick CVB

Quebecor World

RICPCU (Rhode Island Chapter Chartered Property Casualty Underwriters Society)

RIHIMA (Rhode Island Health Information Management Association)

Rhode Island Hospitality Association

Sail America

St. George's School

Salve Regina University

SCFEA (South Carolina Festival and Event Association)

SeaWorld Orlando

Simmons College

Sinclair Communications

Southwest Airlines

State Street Bank

Stop & Shop Women's Leadership Conference

Texas Fairs & Events Association

TFEA (Texas Festival and Events Association)

Three Rivers Community College

TIA (Travel Industry Association of America)

TRPA (Texas Recreation and Parks Association)

University of Rhode Island GSLIS (Graduate School of Library and Information Studies)

University of Rhode Island MBA Program

University of Rhode Island PSPD (Planning Services and Professional Development)

Urban County Leadership

US Army

Woodlands Town Center Improvement District

To book Gail for your corporation, association or conference, please contact gail@gailspeaks.com. Website: gailspeaks.com

About Gail Lowney Alofsin

Gail Lowney Alofsin is an author, professional speaker, adjunct professor, humanitarian, and sales and marketing executive.

A graduate of Tufts University where she majored in Political Science, Gail had the privilege of studying in Tailloires, France and London, England in addition to a summer backpacking through Europe. She has a certificate in Leadership from Bryant University.

Gail has worked for Newport Harbor Corporation since 1988 in several roles - operations, business development, sales, marketing, public relations, event development and management, food and beverage, corporate sponsorship and experiential marketing. Under her leadership, corporate sponsorship sales were increased by 5700%. She has worked on events such as the ESPN Extreme Games, Tall Ships, Health Magazine Feel Great Festival, Sports Illustrated 50th Anniversary Tour, Polar Seltzer Great Chowder Cook-Off, Stop & Shop Taste of Rhode Island, Nantucket Nectars Sunset Music Series, and the Newport International Boat Show, in addition to producing hundreds of corporate events, yacht rendezvous and weddings.

Gail has been an adjunct professor at the University of Rhode Island (URI) since 1999. In addition to teaching in three different departments, Journalism, Public Relations and Communications Studies, she has also created seminars on Work Life Integration and Business Communication for the URI MBA students and Networking and Personal Branding for the URI Career Center. She was featured on the cover of *The Mercury* (oldest newspaper in the United States) for her teaching style which combines real life with core curriculum. Her classes focus on the integration of communication, marketing, public relations, social media and digital literacy, welcoming business professionals as guest lecturers, "real world" experts, and mentors.

Gail leads workshops and speaks at national and international conferences on the topics of Leadership, Sales Success, Marketing, Work/Life Balance and Integration, Personal Branding, Team Building, Customer Service, Spirit in the Workplace and the Power of Positivity. (See AMP!)

A passionate advocate for those less fortunate, Gail serves as a Board of Director for the Martin Luther King Jr. Center and St. Michael's Country Day School. Past board appointments include: United Cerebral Palsy, Leukemia Society, Newport Public Library, the Sovereign Bank Rhode Island Advisory Board and 10 years on the Newport County Convention and Visitors Bureau board.

Gail is an active and dedicated volunteer for her family's non-profit organization, the Haitian Health Foundation (HHF). She has been fundraising for HHF since 1982, and has been volunteering in Haiti on an annual basis since 1983. She resides in Newport, Rhode Island and travels whenever possible with her pilot husband, John and son, Samuel, a left handed pitcher.

About the Haitian Health Foundation

"The worst poverty is the lack of ability to imagine a tomorrow any different from today. The worst poverty is hopelessness. The gift we bring to the poor is the gift of hope."

-Dr. Jeremiah Lowney

From our earliest years, my father and mother reminded us that it was an "accident of birth" that we were born with many privileges and opportunities versus a life of destitution.

When I was a sophomore at Tufts University, I received the news that my father, Dr. Jeremiah Lowney, was diagnosed with cancer and had less than one year to live. Four months following his surgery, my father had the opportunity to serve the poor in Port-au-Prince, Haiti. Soon after this visit, he was asked by Mother Teresa of Calcutta to build a medical clinic in Jeremie, Haiti. This outpatient clinic, built by my mother and father, has served over 200,000 people per year in Jeremie and 102 surrounding villages for over three decades. From the residential Center of Hope for malnourished children and at-risk pregnant women, the St. Pierre School for students (K-7) to development projects (houses, latrines, give-a goat), it is the centerpiece of their projects in Jeremie.

The Haitian Health Foundation and its many generous benefactors bring the gifts of health, education, and hope to thousands of Haitians, trapped in poverty, by no fault of their own.

To help our humanitarian outreach, send your tax deductible donation to:

Haitian Health Foundation
97 Sherman Street, Norwich, CT 06360
www.HaitianHealthFoundation.org

Mesi anpil! (Creole for *"Thank you very much."*)

ACKNOWLEDGMENTS

I am blessed with the gift of very positive people in my life with many to thank in regard to commencing and completing this book. I am grateful for my family, friends, clients, colleagues, interns, students, and the people who I have had the privilege to meet through working, teaching and speaking throughout the years.

Growing up in our family, my parents berated "big talkers." I offer my sincere and deepest gratitude to my parents, Jeremiah and Virginia Lowney, for making us accountable. When we commenced a project, sport, or activity, we completed it, from start to finish, even if we did not enjoy or excel at it.

I thank my parents for the "no complaining" rule in our household. *"Accentuate the positive,"* was a quote I often heard, coupled with *"Your attitude determines your altitude."*

I thank them for not allowing me to waste time complaining about a pimple, a bad grade, a quarrel with a friend or being bored (God forbid!).

I thank my parents for keeping their four children involved with positive activities – family vacations, board games, lessons (swimming, art, piano, etc…), exercise, 5K road races, and family time.

I thank them for inspiring lifelong learning.

My mother has always counseled us not to waste time arguing with family or friends. She feels life is too short for altercations and used to start singing *"Let There Be Peace On Earth"* when we squabbled as siblings. She has given us the gift of a family who loves and supports each other.

I appreciate my brother, Dr. Mark Xavier Lowney, who is an exemplary husband, family man, brother, humanitarian, and doctor. I have respect and admiration for his deep faith. He is the first to help other people and is raising five outstanding children – Zachary, Brennan, Arianna, Ashton and Zoe with his beautiful (inside and out) wife Kristine. They are excellent parents and best friends. They certainly manage their time to garner the most out of life.

I am simply in awe of my sister, Dr. Jennifer Lowney and her ability to "do it all" while making it look seamless. In addition to working full time in her profession as a skilled and personable orthodontist (her operatory is so relaxing and fun – you look forward to your appointment!), she is an excellent wife and mother. Her husband, Rick, is an organizational genius and a master in his field of max-illofacial surgery. Together they are raising four lovely young ladies – Cassidy, Madison, Paige and Sydney, the latter three are triplets. At one point they had four daughters under the age of three. I learn a new organization method from Jennifer and Rick every time I am with them.

My sister, E. Marilyn Lowney, executive director of the Haitian Health Foundation, is a leader and humanitarian gifted with empathy and a great capacity to love. She is the first to take the shirt off her back for others – completely selfless and altruistic. She is an example of impressive organization and is the ultimate "packing pro." In addition to over three decades of travelling to Haiti together, we have also travelled to China, Thailand and Morocco, to name a few of our "magical mystery tours." Her *"Mary Poppins"* bag, while small and portable, is always full of everything and anything you would need. If I did not know better, I would think that she was Samantha Stephens of the America sitcom *"Bewitched,"* wiggling her nose to produce all the items she packs within limited space.

The gift of time has been afforded to me by my mother-in-law, Ruth, whether it is creating incredible dinners or ironing Sam's shirts. I am most appreciative to have a mother-in-law that I love and adore. I have never taken this for granted. Peace in the family is an ultimate time saver. Now, if I could only learn how to cook like she does! Scrumptious!

Faith has a way of putting everything into perspective with the realization that we are here, on this earth, to make the most out of the hours we are blessed with. I am grateful for Sister Theresita Donach ("Sister T"), who has remained pivotal in my life since meeting her as my 8th grade teacher at the impressionable age of 13. She reinforced the foundation of faith set by my parents. I am most appreciative of the spiritual education she shares to this day. Trust in God, sharing our blessings with others and sincere gratitude for what we have been given is the supreme time saver!

Abby Murphy has been a pillar of peace and growth for me. I met Abby in 1988 when I commenced my career with Newport Harbor Corporation. She has a gift for inspiring others and has encouraged me through my event marketing, speaking, teaching and writing careers. Abby also demonstrates, on a daily basis, that through simplicity, we are able to understand how much we truly have.

I would be remiss not to mention my "Haiti" friends – Kathryn Whitney Lucey, Colleen Hopkins and Kathryn Farrington who have been supportive of our Haitian Health Foundation project and of my personal endeavors for over two decades. True friends are hard to come by - many thanks for your support, perspective and love.

I have had the privilege of working on events and business programs for many corporations, inclusive of the Hatteras Yacht Company. My former client and good friend Rhonda Myers, Boston Yacht Sales, is gifted with the ability to give without the expectation of gain. Always cognizant of others and their interests, she is a friend and mentor to many people.

The ultimate networker, Rhonda introduced me to author and speaker, Sharon Hoyle Weber, over a very vibrant lunch featuring a beautiful view and delicious cuisine at the Mooring Seafood Kitchen and Bar in Newport, Rhode Island. Due to Rhonda's innate listening skills, she knew that I wanted to write a book and that Sharon wanted to garner more speaking engagements. Sharon and I commenced our bi-monthly phone calls in January 2011 to serve as each other's respective "Accountability Coach," reporting in on our progress. Sharon – thank you for glancing through my tote bag full of writing and stating: *"The book is done – just start typing!"*

Writing a book is an arduous task, resembling a puzzle with many pieces to assemble, some more complicated than others. I appreciate the encouragement by author and speaker Brian Butler whom I met while waiting in line at an American Marketing Association (AMA) event. Brian also encouraged me that the book was already written, just start typing.

Another introduction through an AMA meeting was to author, speaker and publishing coach, Patrick Snow. As a member of Patrick's mastermind publishing group, I do my best to phone in monthly to garner inspiration in addition to writing advice. Thank you to the sincere, unselfish and inspirational Patrick Snow!

In March of 1988, I attended my first IEG (International Events Group) Conference where I became a lifelong student of the business of corporate sponsorship and experiential marketing. Thank you to Lesa and Jon Ukman for inviting me to teach at a small round table and subsequently my own room of hundreds of people. Thank you to my IEG friends, inclusive of but not limited to Jim Andrews, Penny Perrey, Bill Chipps, Laren Ukman, Emily Howell Rogers, Michael Archibald and Mike Maggini for their continued support and confidence in my presentations. After two decades, the conference continues to be the educational highlight of my year.

I thank International Festivals and Event (IFEA) President, Steve Schmader, for inviting me to present both "the basics" and advanced information at the annual IFEA conference for close to two decades. The learning and sharing at this conference has been invaluable. Thank you to IFEA's Vice President of Marketing and Communications, Nia Forster Hovde, for welcoming me to present IFEA Webinars and submit magazine articles for IFEA's international publication –i.e. Magazine.

Who knew? Thank you to Dr. Tony Silvia, former Chairman of the Journalism

Department at the University of Rhode Island (URI), for "discovering me" and inviting me to teach in the URI Journalism department in January 1999. From the departments of Journalism to Public Relations and currently Communications, teaching is a highlight of my week. I also thank Dr. Renee Hobbs, Dr. Steve Wood, and Dr. Lynne Derbyshire for their support and warm welcome to the Harrington School of Communication and Media at the University of Rhode Island. And, a very special thank you to my URI mentor, Dr. Agnes Doody.

Thank you to Tony's lovely wife, Gina Silvia, for her insight over the years in regard to teaching and writing. Additionally, I thank Gina for the second round of edits on this book. It is no small feat to edit a book. Her diligence and encouragement during the process was most appreciated.

In 1988, I was hired by Steve Prime to work with a very vibrant team to generate business on four acres of waterfront in Newport – the Newport Yachting Center. What an opportunity! I thank Steve for this entrepreneurial and exciting endeavor. General Manager, Chris Perrotti, taught us that it was okay to make mistakes as long as we learned from them. Under his leadership, a strong foundation was built for the facility and events. Our current General Manager, Michele Maker Palmieri, often states and lives by – *"Oh, but the places we will go,"* leading the current team to bring the Newport Yachting Center to new heights.

I have had the privilege of working for Newport Harbor Corporation (NHC) for over two decades. J. Timothy O'Reilly, our former president, has served as a mentor and friend. Tim led the growth and development of NHC with an iron fist although it did soften throughout the years. Our bi-annual lunches have been an opportunity to learn from an astute businessman and community leader with a very big heart. His generosity to both the employees and the community is an inspiration.

I have had the pleasure of knowing our current NHC President, Paul O'Reilly, for over three decades. One of the many lessons I learned from Paul is the power of focus. Success is the result of focusing on growth initiatives that serve our internal and external customers. I also subscribe to his sage advice – *"clean your desk once a decade."*

Meeting Renata Adams in February, 1996, when I returned from my maternity leave was a gift. Her friendly smile, wisdom and encouragement, especially over our Sunday morning coffees, have been moments that I cherish. I always depart from "Coffee with Renata" ready to achieve the best in life.

I had the privilege of welcoming a student, Kelly Adams, to my class at URI. She introduced me to her father, Mark Adams, who has graced my classroom as a guest speaker and mentor for over ten years. In addition to business and career acumen, Mark is a time management guru especially in regard to "to accomplish" lists.

I have met so many special students through both internships and teaching at the university. I thank you all for your time, enthusiasm, smiles and encouragement.

My Aunt Terry Winiarski Merrill, former Vice President of Marketing for a major airline, is a professional inspiration for myself and many other women. My late Aunt Frances Plourde displayed interest in us from childhood through adolescence, serving as an excellent mentor. As an educator, she inspired the love of teaching in me at a very young age. My late Aunt Joan taught us all many lessons inclusive of *"write a thank you note for a thank you note."* Aunt Fran and Aunt Joan are missed, every day. Aunt Terry, you are appreciated more than you will ever know.

Brian Heil, Legion 13, is responsible for the cover designs and layout of this book. It has been an honor to learn from him at every meeting. Brian is blessed with great talent inclusive of creating the original artwork and graphics for Monster.com. In July 2013, as we were completing the layout for this book, Brian lost his daughter, Shannon, in a tragic automobile accident. Brian's deep faith as we completed the book has served as an inspiration. I am humbled by the legacy of grace that his daughter, Shannon, has left with the many lives that she touched. We have dedicated a page to Shannon in this book. Sunshine and dragonflies.

I had the privilege of working with both Brian Heil and our friend Gary Stiffler,

President of The Matlet Group, on *"But to Serve,"* by Marci Alborghetti. This book was written to document my mother and father's humanitarian work in Jeremie, Haiti. I thank Gary and Brian for their patience with that book and for being interested in working with me on a second. Additionally, Gary and I have served on the Martin Luther King Jr. Center board for many years. He is a true humanitarian — always looking out for the best interests of other people. I am most appreciative of my "Ohio" friend and mentor, Gary Stiffler. Due to Gary's generosity, 100% of the proceeds of the first 1000 copies of this book will be donated to non-profit organizations. Our goal is $25,000.

A special thank you to my friend and former student, Ryan Nolan, for providing advice as I was approaching the "finish line" with this book. Ryan's email read:

"There is a quote by the great David Ogilvy that I thought pertained to the possible grammar mistakes you are worried about making in your book:

I don't know the rules of grammar... If you're trying to persuade people to do something, or buy something, it seems to me you should use their language, the language they use every day, the language in which they think. We try to write in their vernacular. -David Ogilvy

Gail, your book is focused on talking to the everyday person, writing as if you were having a conversation with the reader giving advice, not lecturing. That is what made your class amazing, you realized that you may not know everything but you are constantly learning and spread your knowledge to everyone around you."

Thank you Ryan, after four edits, it is time to let go!

Friends are so important in the fabric of our lives. Instead of listing them individually under acknowledgments and inadvertently forgetting someone, many are included in the "Wisdom" section of the first fourteen chapters entitled: *"What Are You Waiting For?"* If I have forgotten someone, please contact me and let me know that you would be interested in being included in the second edition of this book.

My husband John is "the caulking, the glue," of our family, keeping us organized and moving forward. He is an award winning sailor, brilliant pilot and innate business man. He is kind, generous and empathetic. I have referred to him on several accounts as the "best father." The quality time that he has spent with Samuel from the moment he was born is immeasurable. Through education, baseball, travel and pure enjoyment of time together, they are the best of friends. John is a thoughtful man and my very best friend. Most of the time he tells me what I need to hear versus what I want to hear, which is certainly a crucial time saver! From the words of one of our favorite movies, *Love Actually*, *"God only knows where I'd be without you!"*

Samuel, thank you for being the best son parents could ask for. You are indeed, our world, and we love you beyond measure. This book was written for you. Thank you for being a constant reminder that *"Love is all you need."* Love, that's you.

"Who motivates the motivator?" is a question that I have been asked on several occasions. I thank my husband, John, and our gift of a son, Samuel, for simply being there. This is never a simple thing nor something to take for granted. Thank you for the encouragement, great times together and laughter. You are both, indeed, my whole world, reminding me daily that *"Someday IS now."*

God bless you both.

Your Someday is Now.

Shannon Heil
November 10, 1995 - July 11, 2013

You have all of eternity after you die
to be nothing; to do nothing.

Remember that time won't
stop for you, and that the time
you have left is a mere strike
of lightening compared to the
time you'll have once it's all over.

So allow yourself to be happy
one moment, and sad the
next. Be angry and scared
and confused and excited.

Hold your grip on what you
believe in, and use your voice
whenever you can.

Inhale love,
exhale hate.

It's your story.
Make it worthwhile.
Make it something to remember.

Shannon published this on
her Twitter April 10, 2013

It has been a privilege to work with Brian Heil on the layout and design of this book. On July 11, 2013, Brian lost his daughter, Shannon, in an automobile accident. During the process of designing this book Brian shared the following words from one of Shannon's final twitter posts. Shannon lived her life to the fullest – this page is a tribute to her grace, humility, and spirit.

Notes

Notes

Notes

Notes

Notes